Sign here, here and here!. . .

Journey of a Financial Adviser

By Keith G Churchouse

© *March 2010*

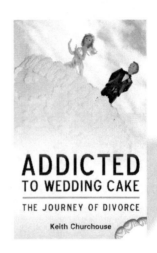

ADDICTED
TO WEDDING CAKE

THE JOURNEY OF DIVORCE

Keith Churchouse

NAGGED,
TAGGED AND BAGGED

THE JOURNEY OF RECOVERY

Keith Churchouse

The Churchouse Chronicles©

The second in the series of *Churchouse Chronicles* is the book,

Journey of Divorce, Addicted to Wedding Cake

www.addictedtoweddingcake.co.uk

Released June 2010
Available in paperback and e-reader ISBN: 978-0-9564325-2-0

Reviews:

'His writing style is easy, informative and light. With just the right amount of humour which never debases, nor makes fun, he creates an atmosphere of understanding. Congratulations! **J.Walker**

'..you can flip to the section that you need advice on or read through it and get a handle on each stage of the process. I have already recommended it to several friends who are divorcing because I really think it will help them.' **Olivia Busnell-Lane**

The third in the series of *Churchouse Chronicles* is the book,

Divorce Recovery, Nagged, Tagged and Bagged

www.naggedtaggedandbagged.co.uk

Released June 2011
Available in paperback and e-reader ISBN: 978-0-9564325-4-4

Review:

'Nagged, Tagged and Bagged offers those who have been through divorce a thought provoking guide to creating a fulfilling future.' **K.Finnis**

Keith Churchouse asserts the moral right to be identified as the author of this Work in accordance with the Copyright, Design and Patents Act 1988.

ISBN 978-0-9564325-0-6

Further contact details and information can be found at www.signherehereandhere.co.uk

No financial advice of any description is offered or deemed to have been provided during the text of this book.

Some of the names, titles, sequencing, areas and dates have been amended to ensure that this work portrays a personal experience rather than those of individuals or companies. Any similarity to individals and groups is purely coincidental. This book is also an expression of the personal opinion of the author on his journey through his work in financial services.

A donation will be made to the charity 'Association for Spina Bifida and Hydrocephalus' for each book sold. Registered Charity No: 249338. www.asbah.org

Acknowledgements

Esther Dadswell

The first acknowledgement has to go to Esther, my wife and fellow director, whose business and engineering prowess have been fundamental in allowing me to produce the text for these pages.

I am grateful for your unrelenting guidance in this task.

Thank you for providing the cash to start the company and I am sorry that I have failed to meet my part of the bargain by not moaning about simply everything!

Thank you also for staying around. I would not have taken the best part of this journey without you.

My parents, Rosamund and Roger Churchouse

You will start to see a common theme here in thanking them for putting up with me.

It's been fun; well, for me anyway!

Thanks for suggesting that I join a bank as that financial services path seems to have worked well for me. And if you have any other challenges for my work career, then I am busy that day!

To my loyal work friends and colleagues

To Alistair G., Gordon B., Steve W., Mike P., Mark C., Michael D., Nick and Martin B. and the others that I am always pleased to hear from.

Thank you for your support, candour, guiding wisdom and professionalism.

You are the pinnacle of what true financial services advice should be about. Without you and others of your kind, UK financial advice would be in a sorry state. Well done. Be bold and keep going.

To the guiding hands that have helped me with this book

Thank you to:

Fiona Cowan, Words That Work,
Contact: fifix@btopenworld.com

Graham Booth, Creation Booth,
Contact: www.creationbooth.com

Jo Parfitt, Creative Mentor,
Contact: www.joparfitt.com

Napier University, Edinburgh

Thank you for allowing me to study at your university. Your course and tutorial style expanded the possibilities of my world and for that I am truly grateful.

And finally my clients past, present and future

My warmest thanks go to you, without whom, I would not have enjoyed my journey through sales advice and financial services.

Thank you.

Foreword

Trust me, I am an insurance salesperson!

This may not provide you with the confidence you require — but is that because of the word *insurance* or *salesperson*?

To some extent we are all sales people in both our personal and business lives. With UK commerce having progressively changed to a service based economy, this has become ever more the case in our society.

Whether you are persuading your child that a trip to the dentist will benefit him or her, and offering a token in return for good behaviour; or a landowner negotiating a large property development; or a commodity trader dealing in coffee options — you are still a salesperson, following the same principles of sales rules and the fundamentals of supply and demand. It just a question of how you get there.

This work looks at the principles of sales in UK personal financial services. It reveals, in some cases, the surprising and amusing ways that sales can manifest themselves and the pitfalls that you should look out for.

We have seen a great deal of change in regulation and governance in all professions, which affects the business we produce and its management. In the case of retail financial services, many people are forecasting even greater change in within the next few years. I will look at middle management and highlight the frustrations that are generated as you mature through your career, striving for success. You may recognise these growing pains in yourself — and through this, learning inspiration can enable you to make a positive difference to your achievements.

As your career develops, you may decide to take the plunge and start your own business. Would you have enough inner knowledge to undertake this leap of faith? I will point out the advantages and issues you may expect to face.

Over nearly a quarter of a century the principles of sales — in all industries, financial services and beyond — have not changed, although the trends and fashions we live in are constantly changing. From Presidents Gorbachev and Reagan to the current incumbents, the rules of political engagement seem little changed from 1985 to date, although their importance remains constant. This may be the same for other areas, such as the music scene, as you will see.

Sales, as a career in any field, is a challenging prospect. Successful sales people need to maintain the colours of a chameleon, adapting to the scenarios they face. Next time your spouse or partner, family member or friend remarks that you are in sales for 'XYZ' company, you might invite them to read this book. They might then realise that the salesperson they refer to is a counsellor, entrepreneur, business person, accountant, actuary, and *finally* salesperson all rolled into one.

Whatever you do, in whatever role you find yourself or evolve into on your own journey, be good at what you do and make a difference. Add something valuable to your world. It makes life easier and the income gained becomes a consequence rather than a target.

Contents

Sign here, here and here!...

1. Bring a bottle and a large amount of cash

My objective in writing this book is to share experiences, with a few chuckles along the way, and possibly to get you out of a scrape or two. Most of all, I hope the book will help you to strive and excel at your chosen goals, whether they are in financial services or any other type of sales or work environment.

Everyone remembers their first sale. Do you remember the first time you were sold to? I do.

The picture of the F14 Tomcat fighter bomber, launching from an aircraft carrier with full afterburners on, could still be seen in the faded model box as I gazed up across the chocolate counter. A rather presumptuous but nevertheless effective sales opportunity presented itself to the salesman behind the counter and he pounced.

'An excellent model and one I am sure would work well with any collection you have at home,' he exhaled as he reached up to the box in a cocksure manner and blew away some of the dust as it entered my grasp. I had been saving up for something else but the lure of the coloured transfers in the kit were too much to resist.

'Would you like it in a bag?' he asked as he moved both me and the box towards the till. Before I could utter an objection the cash, my only savings, had been exchanged for the bag and I was standing outside the antiquated Pangbourne newsagent's shop I had entered only five minutes earlier. I was ten years old and the cocky salesman was my own brother, aged twelve.

The reality of most things in life is that they need to be *sold* at some time, even if it is only the sale of a model aircraft to gain additional shelf space! The definition of a *sale* could read as 'the creation of a contract between two or more parties for something to occur or to change hands'. The law of supply and demand has existed since the year dot.

A simple sale can be the transfer of a product in return for a cash sum, something that happens in our shops every second. The *product* can be anything from a small chocolate bar to a television — but a *sale* can refer to most things, including property and financial services.

The purchase process can be complicated and this why you need a *salesperson*.

The salesperson can appear in various shapes and sizes and have different titles, such as Negotiator, Sales Executive or even Financial Planner.

These sales people also appear at different times in your life; from the person selling you a school uniform as a youngster, to a financial adviser that offers an equity release plan to those of more mature years.

The first salesperson you encounter may be one of your own parents. They have to *sell* you various ideas and concepts that you may not want to accept as a youngster, unless bribed accordingly. For example you might be coaxed into a trip to the dentist, on the understanding that if you behave during your treatment you will get your favourite meal or the DVD you craved this month.

If you accept this deal (or *bribe*, if you want to call it that) the sale is complete.

As you grow older, the same process occurs again and again.

You may have to decide which university you *buy* into, or which pension you buy to invest for your retirement, or which houses you buy during your travels through life. Each of these is a decision involving a *contract* between you and another party.

In undertaking this contract, you aim to get what you want at the price or format you negotiated, and the salesperson (the course leader or tutor, the financial planner or representative, the negotiator) achieves the sale and an addition to his or her overall target.

Even education is target led!

For a good salesperson, there is nothing like meeting your sales target or achieving that elusive 'big deal' sale that you have been working on for the last eight months. You know the one I mean. I'm sure you have one in your own sales pipeline at the moment, that will be the difference between you meeting your bonus or not, or pushing you to the top of the sales league, if that's what is important to you. The adrenaline rush of doing this deal is something to be savoured.

But at what cost has that sale been made — and whom does your advice serve best?

Does it mainly serve that pushy middle-manager who has to tick a Key Performance Indicator (KPI) box on your employer's management information system, in order to announce to the sales director: 'Look how well I have done with our sales team'?

Or was it for the client and his or her best interests?

I always ask the question: 'If this were my relative sitting in front of me — wife, mother, father, even my doting granny — knowing all the facts, would I ask *them* to sign here, here and here?'

If the answer is no, then it's time to think again.

Before you think about which company you represent, always remember that you will always represent *yourself* first. That's the most important thing, both now and in the future. One key point that will course through this book is that 'people buy people'. In a sale the client buys *you* and what you personally represent first, before he buys your product. Never underestimate the power of 'you'. The subliminal message that you carry should be reflected in all your business activities, including your marketing materials, your branding and the way you dress. This is covered in more detail later in the book.

However, this introduces the issue of *passion* to make a good quality sale, and your desire to achieve. If the answer to the question about making the sale above is *yes!*, then both you and the client need to know it is the right thing to undertake.

Also, is the selling you undertake a true sale or just an order-take? Let me explain.

Most of us agree that cars can be an emotive subject for some people. For these people the right car can evoke great passion. If they have sufficient funds, and it is obvious that they already have the desire when they enter a showroom, will they buy? *Yes!* And is that salesperson taking an order or selling a car?

If he or she sells only the car, then it is an order-take. Faced with this level of customer desire, he or she should be able to sell a service warranty, insurance, finance, interior and exterior aftercare, and so on. That would be a true *sale*.

Isn't this sale easier when you have a tangible product that can be felt, touched, caressed and even sat in? What about a non-tangible product, such as a pension, investment or insurance? How does this change the process of the initial sale to the completion of the deal, and a payment into the bank?

Before you read any more of this book, let's get one thing straight: this is not a bunch of notes on how to be ethically superior to your peers. I have no right to do that. It is purely a journey, *my* journey to be precise, through 25 years of providing financial services advice and the experiences — both professional and personal — of my travels through my profession.

I hope you are ready to share the rollercoaster ride that follows. This record considers how altering economic climates, financial issues, regulation and sales situations have manifested themselves and changed over time in this ever-evolving and dynamic world in which I have worked and lived.

In reading these chapters, you may also ask yourself: 'If he's so good at what he does, how has he found the time to write a book?' This is a very fair question, which I would like to answer with another question: 'How have you found time to read it?'

A testament to the control you apply to your time management and business prowess is finding the time to fulfil your desire for development in your field of expertise.

If I can offer you a few shortcuts to sales success from my financial advice and sales experience, or even a little peace of mind and wellbeing, then this work will have been worth it — for both of us, both reader and author.

I fear this may disappoint one or two of you who were hoping to find *The Bluffer's Guide to Flogging Policies*. It is not that — but it will provide you with intelligent thoughts on the navigation of financial services, provision of advice, and the changing challenges at the coalface of sales and advice.

The text covers a myriad of areas and subjects. It ranges from who *you* really are, through financial services sales experience and training, to management styles, regulation and starting your own business.

You will find many learning points for yourself, either suggesting what you should look for in your own career or, alternatively, helping you observe and understand what is happening in someone else's work experience — and these are things that you may want to help with, or to avoid at all cost.

Although related to financial services, these thoughts are relevant to any individual, organisation or industry that involves pre-sales advice, sales and after-sales service. Bearing in mind that this usually covers the whole of industry, this should make for very relevant reading no matter what industry you work in.

Non-delivery of the goods, product or service you have promised a customer can be embarrassing at best and expensive at worst. Take the sale/bribe example, with the child going to the dentist. Imagine if *your* child got short-changed on the DVD/favourite meal deal. I would not want to be in the room when that 'deal' collapsed, especially after the dentist's drill. Delivery of the goods or service is what any sale is about, whether that be a physical product, such as a car, or a non-tangible expectation of future prosperity, such as a pension offered from a financial planner.

It all becomes more interesting — and complicated — at the *non-tangible* part of the sale.

Within the world of financial advice we have regulation from the Financial Services Authority (FSA) and I will consider this at various points in the next few chapters. Regulation does not guarantee that the sale will achieve the client's expectations. It should mean that the sale was completed within the boundaries of the relevant regulation at that time — and we all know that regulation changes over time.

The non-tangible sale involves managing client expectations of what can be achieved with the current assets and time available. Being there in person at the end of the contract may be difficult if the non-tangible product reaches maturity at the client's age 65. This might be in 40 years' time. That does not stop you endeavouring to ensure that everything is in place now, to meet those expectations in four decades' time.

If the client happens to be a family member, you may well be around in person at the retirement party to see the fruits of your advice, so make sure you get it right now or you might be invited to bring a bottle . . . and a large amount of cash!

Taking this point further, I am not an advocate of providing financial advice to relatives and friends.

By the time of maturity, even the best financial advice and product may not turn out to be what had been anticipated, and this can often be in many years' time. An obvious example is endowment policies that may have performed very well for many years but, as the economy changed, ultimately fell short of expectations.

I once witnessed a sales manager suggesting that his team go home and sign up their families. *Don't!* The manager will be long gone by the time the product matures — and you may still be there. In my opinion, this is usually a sign of a manager's desperation, rather than good marketing and advice.

In the rest of this book, I believe you will learn something new, or uncover an old value or quality that you had forgotten.

Trust me. I'm an insurance salesman!

Chapter 1 in a nutshell

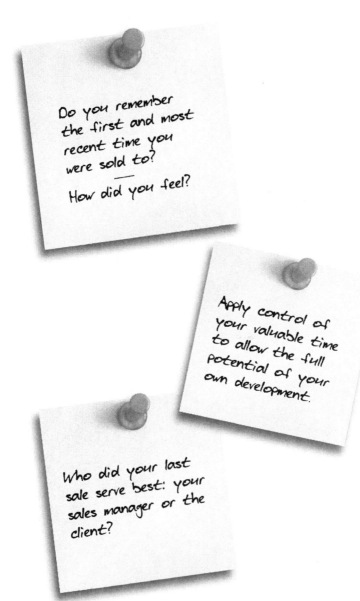

Do you remember the first and most recent time you were sold to?
—
How did you feel?

Apply control of your valuable time to allow the full potential of your own development.

Who did your last sale serve best: your sales manager or the client?

Sign here, here and here!...

2. That sales motivator

No one knows you like you do

I was about to confirm at this point that your confidence in your sales ability and process is everything — but on reflection, that is too simplistic.

Confidence, attitude, charisma, intelligence, communication and ability must comprise the overall focus, *your* overall focus, for success in whatever field you find yourself. You need to understand which of these above areas you personally need to develop, and then work hard on that area to be the best.

You may wish to tell me that you are already great in all of these areas, which is fine. However, I suspect you would not be reading this book if you weren't motivated to improve your position. Everyone can. The person who stops learning and developing loses focus and the likelihood of success.

So, what type of person are you really?

Are you forward and outgoing? The quiet determined type? Shy and retiring? (Which may not be the ideal characteristics for working in a face to face sales or advice process.) Are you gregarious and full of energy? Clearly, this is not an exhaustive list; we are each unique, coming from different backgrounds and having experienced varying cultures, religions, geography and journeys.

Your individual character and energy are everything in face-to-face sales 'combat'. This also applies to financial services advice, just as it does in any of the fields of personal and direct communication, such as the armed services — except that in sales and advice we're not issued with tanks! You may also want to hold on to the hard hat and flak jacket for those awkward missions into your client bank, to ensure that your motivation to win the sale will sustain you in the face of a client's initial objections.

Never forget that the biggest weapon in your arsenal is your *smile*. Yes, I did say that: your smile. Try using it. A smile can be very powerful, breaking many an intense sales situation and overcoming objections you may face in your field of work. They can also be infectious for your clients.

Thinking of client buying objections, I was once taught that if a client falters at proceeding with a purchase then you should list out the client objections with him or her. You then seek to answer these points, one by one, to allay each concern. The last objection listed by the client is usually the one that, once overcome, will make them buy.

Satisfiers and dis-satisfiers: what motivates you?

We are all different. However, it is sometimes easy to forget that so are our clients.

You may already have found out the hard way that each of your clients has varying personal motives for your contact with them — and that those motives can vary even between partners in a personal relationship. This can be anything from wanting to save for an event in six months' time, to investing for the future education or an inheritance for the grandchildren. But what emotion lies behind this, which drives the motive? It's quite amusing to pose the same question to spouses or partners in front of each other, and to get opposite answers at the same time. The uncomfortable looks between the parties can tell many stories.

A young and dynamic unmarried couple came to see me in Guildford about an inheritance the man had received. Toby and Sarah were considering the planning for this money and I asked if they planned to marry.

'Yes!' Toby answered immediately, a broad smile sweeping over his bespectacled face.

'Is that a proposal?' Sarah smiled, blushing at the situation and his level of commitment to her.

'I suppose it might be,' he responded sheepishly.

You see, a good adviser can be a matchmaker as well. Well, almost. And yes, they are now happily married!

Clients have motives behind their ambitions — but what are *your* motivations? The simplest answer is: money. Surely every salesperson would agree. But is it really? And if it is money, then why money? Does money afford you the ability to keep your family in a nice house, have a fast car or boat or motorcycle, or to keep your darling offspring in private education? One recent remark I heard was, 'He who dies with the most toys wins!'

As an alternative to money, are you motivated by status? Status can be a powerful motivator for many people. I have to say that it is a motivator for me, although this seems to be waning as I get older.

If your motivation is status, again the question has to be: why? Are you the proverbial 'control freak' who has to rule all you survey and, in addition, wants to control other people? Or do you want to be involved in the management and structure of a company? And will your contribution add to the success of this structure? In what way? Or is it something else? Are you just driven to do better, whatever role you have?

Likewise, what *de-motivates* you? There could be a number of issues. Is it your company car? Your office conditions and desk position? Perhaps it's the lack of recognition of or even interest in your work within the organisation? Or, as a final example, is it the rigid confines of the management structure that you work in? Think about it: what upsets and really grinds you? It may be a combination of these or other situations.

If you find you have a list, you will usually find that the last point you note is the one that irritates you the most.

Once you have identified the main issue then, above all, you need to focus on how to control that negative position that it promotes. How is this going to fit into the planet that will be your sales universe for the next 10-20-30 years, if you are going to make a career of it? Whatever you decide, make sure that it is not enough to distract you from your overall goal, and put you off completely.

Taking this point a stage further, Frederick Irving Herzberg (1923–2000) talks about 'hygiene factors' (dis-satisfiers) and 'motivators' (satisfiers) in his 1968 publication *One More Time, How Do You Motivate Employees?* As an observation, he states that pay and benefits are not motivators, but hygiene factors.

Also significant is Maslow's *Hierarchy of Needs* (Abraham Maslow in his 1943 paper *A Theory of Human Motivation*).

If you take nothing else from this book, then please read the basic notes of both of these works. They are both brilliant studies and highly relevant to our present day understanding. Some would argue that they are now outdated; I disagree.

They will show you that the frequent frustrations you experience have all been observed and documented, and the works demonstrate a structure that can help you understand the situation for yourself. Once you have read them and understood the benefits of both studies, leave a copy on your manager's desk to help with his or her understanding and 'skills'.

Morning, governor

This is an important point in your overall strategy: at what time of day do you work best?

I am not sure whether maturity helps a person understand this but I have concluded that I am a morning person. As an example, when undertaking an Honours degree course,

I found that I could concentrate and write at my optimum level in the early morning, say from 5.00 - 10.00 am.

After that, the distractions of the day would become far more exciting, and by 6.00 pm all I wanted to do was relax.

Some successful people have used this to their advantage, realising that you can work from 7.00 - 9.00 am without telephone or email interruptions.

Other people are simply useless in the morning and only become fully focused in the afternoon. There is nothing wrong with this as long as it is understood by the individual concerned. You can spot them round the room in the early morning sales meeting, run by that possibly oafish sales manager. Be aware of this next time it happens. Have a look around the room and grade your colleagues into three categories: Morning, Afternoon or Evening people. Now grade yourself.

Think about this carefully and understand it, because it is vital to your success and personal wellbeing. If you are a morning person and you have a big deal to close, make the appointment for the morning where you will have your sales advantage. If you are like me, don't shoot yourself in the foot and book the appointment at 5.00 pm when you are beginning to wonder where your dinner is.

Also, some individuals like to be the *hunter*, always looking for the new sales opportunity; this is what gives them the thrill and satisfaction. They may find looking after an existing client bank tiresome. Others prefer to *farm* an existing client bank created by previous hunters, rather than seeking sales from new grounds or unbroken areas. You need to take into account whether you are a *hunter* or a *farmer* and adjust accordingly. Remember that both are valuable skills.

Also remember that your well meaning colleagues (and clients to a lesser extent) can be unwitting *time stealers* at crucial points in your business day, such as when you are outside your performance time zone. As an example, if a colleague is a morning person he might ease off in the afternoon and want to chat. Make sure that you are not party to the time stealers and, most important of all, don't become one.

Grubby little industry

In my time, I have met a few people socially who warned me with some conviction that in their 'opinion', financial services and the provision of retail financial advice is 'a grubby little industry'. Not many people say that they set out to be an insurance salesman or financial adviser as their lifelong calling — I know I didn't. I hope that by the time I have finished my career in financial services these people who shared their precious wisdom with me will realise how very wrong they are about the service we can offer.

I write this at a time when financial advisers have been demoted from the top five of most disliked and reviled occupations in the UK, along with estate agents, double glazing sales people, second hand car sales people and ambulance-chasing litigators. These occupations are now being usurped by bankers and MPs jostling for the top spot. In at Numbers One and Two with the credit crunch, recession and the MPs' expenses scandal, I am sure that they will spend many a happy year as the target of ridicule and barbed jokes. 'Enjoy the experience,' is all I can offer as guidance.

The House of Commons has introduced into common usage the word 'redact'. It means: *To make ready for publication; edit or revise*, referring to MPs' public disclosure of expenses and the blacking out of the juicy bits. Will this farce never end? Or should I 'redact' that comment? This word 'redact' has been in the English language since medieval times (1350-1400 AD), and about the same time the word 'expenses' first appeared. Maybe this has been going on longer than we think; in the history of words 'expenses' and 'redact' sit comfortably between 'Parliament' (1250-1300 AD) and 'recession' (1640-1650 AD).

Sadly, it's possible that this demise in the trust of our political leaders will allow other more extreme political groups to manifest themselves in the UK and Europe and gain respectability to cloak their views that may eventually drive us in the wrong direction. This may be the real cost of those expenses scandals.

The reality of providing good quality financial advice is that it can be the most rewarding career available, if you do it correctly. This is partly because of what you do, but mainly because people are fascinating and getting to know them is great fun within the framework of UK regulation.

Regulation is nothing new and it's good for participant protection. The regulation of financial services is here to stay and the regulatory burden will only ever increase as the need for advice expands. This is not an issue and should be embraced because it is a natural part of all walks of life.

Most importantly, you are helping your clients to achieve their aspirations both now and into their long term future. Remember that, as you read the following pages. It's like sitting with someone you don't know at a wedding breakfast and coming to understand them over the next two hours while you enjoy your meal. Do you make it work for you, or do you get bored? That's your call.

Life is about expectations, what you make of it and what you want to achieve. During your life you will receive tutorials in all manner of subjects — but it is the combination of these and the practical experiences of using this learning thereafter that will meet your initial expectations and hopefully surpass them.

The next chapter is all about my experiences and provides some traveller's tales about the journey.

Chapter 2 in a nutshell

Continually develop your sales abilities. The person who stops learning and developing loses out!

Understand what truly motivates you and also what really annoys you. These things are essential for your future in financial services.

Read both
One More Time, How Do You Motivate Employees? By Frederick Irving Herzberg and
A Theory of Human Motivation by Abraham Maslow.

Providing financial advice is one of the most rewarding and satisfying careers, if you apply yourself correctly. You are limited only by your own expectations.

3. What cannot be taught, only experienced

My journey starts in Leatherhead on a cold morning in December 1985 and brings you right up to date. A high-mileage quarter of a century in various sectors of retail financial services work. Whatever you think of her politics, I am sure that Margaret Thatcher would have been proud of me: it was her regime that expanded the UK from a manufacturing base to a services based economy, encouraging heavy investment into the financial services sector. In the current economic climate, that significant change may not have been for the best — however, hindsight is a wonderful thing.

To put these thoughts into context, do you remember late 1985? Here are some reminders:

- President Mikhail Gorbachev of the Soviet Union and President Ronald Reagan of America had their first vital meeting in Geneva to create a 'safer world'

- 60 people died on a hijacked Egypt Air flight in Malta

- Further terrorist attacks followed in December in both Rome and Vienna

- You may have been dancing to Shakin' Stevens at the office Christmas party

- I had sold my first car, a VW Beetle and was now the proud owner of a rusty white Triumph TR7 convertible with a leaking roof.

These random memory joggers make you realise the breakneck but sustained speed with which the world and its economy has developed in the last 25 years.

Consider the irony that at the time of writing this book, President Obama and President Medvedev of Russia have recently signed a nuclear weapons reduction programme. What goes around comes around! Will I see you in 2034 for the next round of armament agreements?

I start this journey through financial services by stating that it is important to note the things that cannot be taught, only experienced. It is a great privilege to work with clients and their finances and to be involved in their intricacies and most precious secrets. What other career offers you the opportunity to meet a new person, usually a good few of them in a week, and within ten minutes of meeting them you are firing personal questions at them about everything from their salary, to health, to their partner's income, to their children and back again?

Secret (and not so secret) mistresses and partners, Swiss bank accounts, serious ill health, death, divorce, births, unknown bank accounts all come out in our questioning. It is a real privilege and honour to see and be involved in — but also a great professional and personal responsibility to care for the client and his or her future.

I will take this opportunity to say thank you to my clients — past, present and into future — first of all for their trust, but also for sharing their lives with me and allowing me to help them.

It does not matter how much sales training and coaching you go through and how many exams you take, time and experience will engulf anyone's career. Nothing can prepare you for the time when a client asks you about *you* rather than them. When the relationship starts to switch over the years from their insurance or pensions person to a friend and confidant, then this becomes a highly satisfying experience.

What I have also observed is that the most successful people and clients are not wealth-focused. Money was not their motivator. Some were born into money, some had personal savings and some had none. However, the successful few knew their trade or profession, became expert at it, and worked solely in that area. Their wealth was not generated from their desire to earn; it was as a consequence of their desire to excel in their chosen field. The money was purely a pleasing by-product of their productivity and focus.

Don't misunderstand this last statement. We are all very different and treat our finances with similar diversity. I have met clients who watch every penny, who guard every second of every minute.

I met a client, Dorothy, who had retired and had significant sums invested in a personally selected portfolio of shares. Dorothy enjoyed good health and was rather austere in her approach. Her home was poorly decorated and the red carpet was threadbare as I sat on a rather rickety 50's style chair in the lounge. Bearing in mind that the carpet and the decor had not changed for 30 years, this situation was rather conflicting and somewhat surprising. Having maintained a high powered job in the past with income to match, she could hardly make eye contact as Dorothy watched her share holdings moving in real time on the gleaming 50-inch plasma screen that dominated the 1970s wallpaper adorning the walls. Did this really make sense? What type of life was she planning for retirement? Had she not missed the point?

Let me dispel any doubt; the answer is *yes*. The reality of life *had* escaped her! Her purpose had become money generation, rather than the rewards that money could provide for her. I understand that some people prefer to live modestly — but this was not the case here.

For some clients, the *consequence* of the income from their toil seemed to be both a surprise and something of a novelty, rather than an expected recognition of their hard work. These clients had set out in early life to be good at their profession or trade and had kept their *heads down and hours up* ever since. It was only when they came to a financial review and their assets were listed out that they really appreciated what they had amassed. This was not their objective and it did not faze them; all they wanted now was for someone else to manage the fruits of their labours so they could carry on doing what they had always done.

Shared experiences

I plan to share with you the different sales situations and scenarios, both serious and amusing. These are good, bad and different situations that cannot be taught; they have to be experienced to help understanding and hopefully to trigger even greater achievement. I believe that this book will touch a few points in your own experiences that you may have had or are yet to enjoy, that make you think: 'Ah yes! I've had that happen too!' or 'I thought it was only me!'

Anyone who has met me will know I can be rather cynical and somewhat scathing at the best of times. Why? I make no apology for this because providing financial advice is quite a 'raw' experience and one that needs to be handled with understanding and care, and also with determination.

What do I mean by that? Ask yourself a question: are you an adviser or a counsellor or both? *Yes, a good adviser is both* should be the answer. Do you map out people's futures and keep them on the straight and narrow? *Yes!* is the answer. Do you endeavour to meet their aspirations and hopes? *Yes!* Do you have to challenge misconceptions and impossibilities? *Yes!*

This is all in a day's work for a good financial adviser. This work has become increasingly relevant in recent times, with the economic turbulence that most people have endured. The benefit of knowing that you are there to support your clients' needs and concerns has never been so important.

Take this a stage further.

A prospect calls to make an appointment to discuss his retirement planning. Terry, a solicitor coming to the end of his working life, is someone I have never met before and we meet to discuss everything about his and his family's needs over the course of a couple of hours. In cases like this you have to test Terry's understanding of himself, challenge any inconsistencies you find, and understand his plans for the future. The normal boundaries of conversation topics disappear as you go on a mutual voyage of discovery, usually with no compass, moral or otherwise.

Clients will take you on a diverse and sometimes fascinating trip. You will need to note down all of this vital and personal information and regurgitate it to him in a written format along with the financial recommendations you are making to match her requirements.

Some clients are exhausted by the process of digging into their innermost thoughts and psyche, aspirations and needs — and sometimes so am I, however fulfilling the process may be. But the reality is that to achieve a good outcome that will stand the test of time, this is what is required. You become hardened to asking awkward questions and the social boundaries you have observed in the past can disappear.

No qualification or exam can teach you this, only time and experience.

The issue of the blunt nature with which you naturally ride over personal boundaries can prove to be difficult in other social situations. When you forget you are not at work, you may unwittingly ask rather forthright conversations, asking for salary details over drinks! This is not recommended; you may end up finding out more about your friends than you really wanted to.

The preamble to my journey ends and we visit 1985 with the next chapter. We start at the end of A-levels with a spotty teenager in Guildford wondering if the world was his oyster.

Chapter 3 in a nutshell

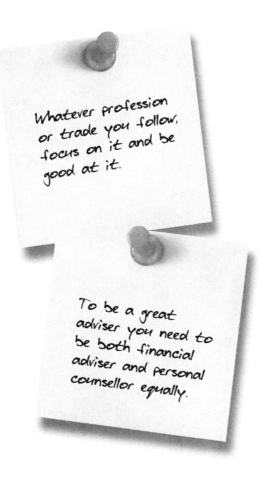

Whatever profession or trade you follow, focus on it and be good at it.

To be a great adviser you need to be both financial adviser and personal counsellor equally.

Sign here. here and here!...

4. The long journey of experience begins

Back in 1985, I happily left school with five O-levels and two A-levels, in Art and Engineering Drawing. All the family maintained a strong work ethic and university was a questionable option. The O-levels were in social science subjects and can probably be characterised as O-level Smoking, Chasing Girls, Home Beer Brewing, and CSEs in both Sociology and Trimming Your Hair In The Style Of The Bass Guitarist From Kajagoogoo. The New Romantic movement had been in full swing for a few years, lead by big bands such as Spandau Ballet and Ultravox.

The reality is that there were a few real exams passed and yes, I got an 'ology'! My Economics O-level was in Getting Money Off Anybody For A Gallon of Petrol For My VW Beetle, soon to be replaced by the rusty Triumph TR7.

As school and then Sixth Form dragged on, students were encouraged to start making decisions as to their plans for after secondary school, to ensure that we added value to the community we were about to enter. Well, that's what our head of year told us to do, anyway. Unfortunately, my application to eclipse David Hockney as a great artist and painter was rejected and therefore my chosen career after school was to be a draughtsman.

Although I had always loved to draw, you will see later that this ambition did not last long.

At age 18, leaving Sixth Form for the last time was a daunting affair — especially as I had decided that I'd had enough of the education system, and university at that point was not really viable. It was time to face reality and get a job. I had to pay for my nightly socialising somehow, and had begun to notice that my credit balance at the 'Parents' Bank' was getting low.

This is another of life's *opportunity junctions*, where you have to make decisions about your future. Bearing in mind that the decisions I had been making up till then were as hard as 'Which parties should I go to this weekend and in what order?' the decision to get a job was of far greater importance than I had experienced before.

Drawing pretty pictures

After writing fifty different letters to try and get a job, I finally secured my first post as a Trainee Draughtsman in East Molesey in the summer of 1985. I was thrilled (at first anyway) by the thought of designing things and coming up with new ideas. This was also my first real commute, around 20 miles up the A3 and hang a right at Cobham.

In reality, I was allowed to trace parts of buildings. I hated it! Boring work, mundane people and with Computer Aided Design (CAD) just around the corner, and my general dislike of computers at that time (oh, how times have changed!) it seemed a thankless task with limited potential.

To put the computer issue into perspective, Microsoft had not even issued Windows 1.0 by then, although in November 1985 it was just about to be released. My personal money management was not going well at the time, with my salary just about able to cover my overdraft bringing my current account balance to nil on the day I got paid! Something had to change, and it did. Within three months of joining, the company decided to relocate to Hampshire and my job was going with it. Either move or leave became the options. Not a hard choice and this became the first of two redundancies, or *opportunity junctions* as I prefer to call them.

Being made redundant is a strange experience. It has the positive power to reinvigorate you, to allow you to refocus on what you want to do and achieve; on the other hand, at age 18, it makes you realise that your ambitions have been shattered. I hadn't a clue what I wanted to do, as I'd only ever wanted to be a draughtsman, and that was boring!

My father, Roger, was manager for a retail bank locally and had been a bank employee man and boy. We, as a family, had grown up with the bank in the background, moving from town to town every seven or so years following his latest appointment.

'Join a bank!' he exclaimed, I think in desperation to ensure that I would not be a drain on his finances after the loss of my job.

'All right,' I bleated sulkily, 'but I'm not joining yours! I'll do it off my own back.'

You will note my stubborn streak throughout the course of this text. You may also observe that the stubborn streak merely transforms into cynicism with the passage of time.

As an aside, the bank that was my father's branch has since become a Jamie Oliver restaurant. Still, at least it's not a trendy wine bar!

Retail banking

In the nick of time, I secured a new job with a local bank.

One Friday morning in 1985 I left the draughtsman job in East Molesey and on the Monday morning became a Grade 1 Assistant at a High Street bank in Leatherhead. At least it was a shorter commute.

What a great first week, with the office Christmas party on the Friday following my start. It was an official function with party games at the end. I am sure that dressing up the (male) Assistant Manager as a woman with bright red lipstick did not help my career prospects, but I was under orders from the compère and in no position to argue. Dancing to Shakin' Stevens singing *Merry Christmas Everyone* soon diverted their attention.

This might have been one of the first years you played Trivial Pursuit whilst gorging on a mince pie and watching the Queen's Speech.

Now, that's not going to teach us anything, but I did meet a colleague at the bank who was to have a profound effect on my future. There have been a few people who steered my thoughts and plans for the future, and not all of them for positive reasons. This person was one of the first.

The main advantage of working in a small retail bank branch was that it required me to learn various roles, which might not have happened in one of the main branches. Another advantage was to gain promotion, to the dizzy heights of Grade 2 Supervisor, within a short time.

The disadvantage was that most of the staff had been there for years and had become entrenched.

'I'm not doing that, that's not my bloody job!' was the cashier's response when I asked for some help in my second week.

Great, I thought, thanks for nothing! I promised myself that if I ever caught myself saying that phrase and meaning it I would have to leave the bank; it never crossed my mind that I too could become a *jobsworth*. I had never really encountered this attitude before and it did not sit well with me.

Looking back now, it made me realise I now had aspirations and parameters, and that I had already set myself up to move onwards and upwards.

As time went on my banking experience extended, although there were some tasks I struggled with. Rupert, the Branch Manager was a super chap, gentle and informed in his style, in the twilight of his career. As a newly trained Supervisor he asked me to open a business account for a client. Now, I had been trained in this procedure twice and still didn't understand how to do it. At the age of 19 and being newly promoted, admitting defeat at the first hurdle did not seem a good option, so I said: 'OK!' The manager gave me a cheque from the client with which to start the account.

We were busy and the cheque sat there all morning, and then all afternoon, to be carefully deposited into my locking top draw for the next day, and the next. After a day or two a few more cheques had arrived. Finally, the manager called me in and sat me down.

'I have another cheque for the new business account. Here it is, have a look.'

The sinking feeling was overwhelming but I kept smiling: 'OK, I'll deal with this.'

'Turn it over,' he requested.

On the back was a message from the client to the manager, requesting the account be *opened*. The note said: 'Rupert, no account open yet. Look into it for me please. Thanks John.'

John, as I found out, happened to be a Senior Manager for the group and was 'Unimpressed of Surrey'.

'Something you want to tell me, Keith?' the manager enquired. My blush matched the crimson carpet. The brightly-striped wallpaper began to feel increasingly like an ominous cage as I regurgitated my errors.

'Um, yes!' I think we ought to go through this account,' I sheepishly replied. I really did feel like a lamb being led to the slaughter.

My strong reprimand was swift and fair and, as you would expect, my additional training was considerably more thorough. No more delayed cheques for me, I can tell you.

Two years later, almost to the day, I said it. I could not believe it came from me.

'I'm not doing that, it's not my bloody job!' I snarled, referring to some trivial matter that needed doing but was clearly beneath me. Since when had I become Lord Muck? The light bulb that went *ping!* above my head was clear enough for me, and I think everyone else, to see. I had no rights to that comment or attitude and certainly did not want to hear these words coming from my own mouth.

My time in the bank had been useful and a good starting point. I had learnt administrative discipline (sadly always worthwhile, if a little dull), met customers, served them and achieved my first career sale — an annual travel policy to an older widowed lady. It was a great feeling.

My sales career had started!

It was a different world then. There were no comparison websites or even the Internet readily available, so the lady's 'shopping around' simply meant visiting the bank and signing up. And as the premium was so high, it met the branch's annual sales target for travel insurance in one go. Wow!

The management were delighted.

That successful feeling and the enjoyment of client-facing contact stayed with me, although in my haste to leave behind my attitude at the bank, the next job in my career would prove to be a wrong turn. Only experience can only teach you that, unfortunately.

My next role was as an administrator for a mortgage group in Hampshire. I think it was my concern that I could become a *jobsworth* that spurred me on, rather than the prospects with the new employer.

The first of two wrong turns in my career was underway.

Chapter 4 in a nutshell

Redundancy can appear to be a desperate time. Use it as an opportunity junction to re-focus on what you want to achieve.

In whatever role you have, know when it is your time to leave.

Never lie to yourself. If the job is wrong for you, then you know it's wrong.

5. Is this the road to a financial services future?

Mortgage administration

I'm not going to dwell for long on this career move. It did have the benefit of teaching me that it was the client contact part of employment that I enjoyed, rather than the administration. You, and you alone, know what appeals to you about an employment position — and it is your gut feeling (usually the first feeling you have) that can tell you this.

One Manager I worked for was great (if somewhat annoying) about knowing what the *gut feel* on a sales case or situation was and whether a profitable conversion was going to occur. In my opinion this was a combination of intuition and experience, which together helped provide understanding of the potential of success. The great thing here is that they were able and prepared to share this combination with any willing ears that would hear and use the message to improve the sales experience for all parties involved. I was lucky enough to enjoy this message at an early stage in my career. I soon found that by paying attention to this intuition you could observe increased sales by applying the same methods in your sales process.

At the age of 21 I was not focused on what I did or did not want from an employment, other than needing to leave the previous employment to get out of the rut. Sometimes, you have to leave somewhere to appreciate the parts of a role that you *did* enjoy. I answered an advert in a local newspaper and came into contact with a recruitment consultant for the first time.

This new role was sold to me by the recruitment agent in Chobham in a pub after work — spot any warning signs? The administration company cared about putting bums on seats, shifting mortgage arrears letters at the rate of ten per hour from a computer. There were computers everywhere; I think even the tea lady had one.

These were the days when mortgage lending had become excessive and debt and arrears were starting to get out of control, with the resulting default notices being posted daily. Does this mortgage arrears situation sound familiar in the current economic climate? I was rather green round the edges and this showed in my lack of questioning to find out whether this new role was going to work for me, rather than just for *them*.

I have to add that this was not the fault of the employer, who had defined the role clearly to the recruitment agent. The employer had seen a huge swell in business in a short period of time, so a volume process had to be applied to ensure that the workload was dealt with. The company maintained teams with team leaders to guide the workload through its requirements.

Unrest within the team was common, usually based on the issue of salary because everyone had been employed on different terms to do the same job. I am not a religious chap — but from memory it sounds a bit like the parable of the Workers in the Vineyard. Clearly this issue of pay, benefits and terms is nothing new.

Within a month I was on the job hunt again, this time with client contact *and* sales in mind. I had identified that I missed the client interaction and sales and this was another personal learning point. This was the clarification that I needed from taking another role.

My brother was a trainee surveyor with a chain of estate agents and business was booming. He let me know that the company he worked for was looking for trainee mortgage brokers; as I was becoming a financial man, this might work for me. I applied, and in April 1988 I started as a trainee mortgage broker in Surrey . . . just before the end of the property boom of 1988-89 and the start of the recession of 1991!

Was it worth the experience? Yes, and I stayed for six years.

The New Romantic era was over (both Spandau Ballet and Ultravox had disbanded) and the summer on '88 beckoned the music of the likes of Bros with *I Owe You Nothing*, which was rather apt I thought wryly, considering the amount of mortgage lending going. The summer saw the Piper Alpha disaster in June.

Mortgage broking

I joined the industry just as the mortgage and housing market was going berserk. This was partly fuelled by Nigel Lawson (Chancellor of the Exchequer at the time) announcing in the Spring 1988 Budget that double MIRAS (Mortgage Interest Relief at Source) was being withdrawn. MIRAS was worth about £60.00 per month to each mortgage applicant or first time buyer; this was a lot of money and was to some extent propelling the residential property market prices into the stratosphere.

For joint mortgage applicants this MIRAS tax relief was worth around £120.00 per month. If anyone tells you that the Budget does not cause an immediate effect on an economy, then read on. The UK housing market and the economy went crazy!

In the time that it takes Nigella Lawson, Nigel's daughter, to crack an egg, my father looked up from the leather chesterfield at the moment Nigel Lawson sat down from his Budget speech and stated: 'You and John [my brother] are moving out!' with a wry grin on his face.

Gulp. My credit balance at the 'Parents Bank' was about to end and the banker was looking to close the current account.

A ten per cent house deposit was miraculously and hurriedly conjured from thin air. This was on loan of course, because my father was still a bank manager and they are not keen on gifts! My brother and I were under offer for a house in Guildford within three days of the announcement at the age of 21, at an agreed price of £66,000 in March 1988.

The market was beginning to move very rapidly and we mail-dropped a local estate with a personal letter asking people whether they wanted to sell their house. A call came within 24 hours and after a mortgage was secured, there was a quick exchange of contracts and we moved in June. The house went up in value by over 20 per cent in four months. We, along with thousands of other applicants, scrambled to get on to the property ladder in time to get the MIRAS benefit, before the August deadline.

I stayed for around eight years and sold the house for . . . just £66,000. When house prices fall as they have done in recent times, don't say we haven't seen it all before!

My financial services career was forming nicely and at this time my new job title was Junior Mortgage Broker. I think 'administrator' would have been more accurate, based on the levels of applications and work coming in, and the lack of available time from the team to train me. Like every other mortgage adviser, they had applicants queuing out of the proverbial door to ensure that they buy their first property before the tax relief door closed — which it did with a resounding clang. They needed to make the most of the glut while it was available. However, eventually, training time was found, and I achieved my first mortgage sale after three months. Excellent!

To put the property sales boom of the late eighties into context, the Tories had won a General Election under Mrs Thatcher in 1987 and the new administration had promised tax cuts. It was down to Nigel Lawson to deliver. Within two Budgets (1987-88) he cut income tax rates from 29p to 25p, while the top rate was cut to 40p. The decreased level of higher rate income tax charge lasted until 2009, with Alistair Darling making the change to 50p from 2010.

In Nigel Lawson's plans for the April 1988 Budget, it is understood that he believed the economy was slowing down at a significant rate — although he also projected a surplus in the future that should justify his income tax cuts and meet the manifesto requirements. This was not to be so. Economic growth was accelerating and the tax cuts and interest rate cuts gave a huge boost to the housing market, with house prices rising excessively during the course of 1988. Within a few months, interest rates had to be doubled and inflation rose sharply.

The fallout from the property market started shortly after the MIRAS panic-buying had subsided in autumn 1988. Some colleagues who had stayed to enjoy the boom left the industry; some organisations that had bought up chains of estate agents decided that the profit they had enjoyed was not there anymore and was unlikely to return quickly — so they sold up.

These changes really started to sort the men from the boys and those who were going to stand the test of time began to show their mettle.

Chapter 5 in a nutshell

Research your recruitment consultant as well as the employment on offer. Flattery from a poor recruitment consultant is a cheap tactic for placing candidates wherever they can, and getting themselves paid.

Life is hard work; get over it and get on with it!

6. The changing face of regulatory requirements

The new job was going well, with a queue of mortgage applicants outside my boss's rather tired looking office. He made the sale and I undertook the administration, with a short break for a sandwich at lunchtime. The local shop made fresh sandwiches to order and they were like doorstops with anything you fancied inside. They were fantastic.

This employment was before the Financial Services Act 1986, which came into force in mid 1988 along with the introduction of various regulatory authorities, such as the Financial Intermediaries Managers and Brokers Association (FIMBRA) and the Life Assurance and Unit Trust Regulatory Organisation (LAUTRO).

These were replaced — along with some of the activities of other regulators, namely Investment Managers Regulatory Organisation (IMRO) and the Securities and Futures Authority (SFA) — by the Personal Investment Authority (PIA) in 1994.

Subsequently, the PIA was itself replaced by the Financial Services Authority (FSA) in December 2001. The FSA exercises its powers using The Financial Services and Markets Act 2000 as an Act of Parliament, and it remains the UK regulator for insurance, investment business and banking.

There were many regulatory changes during this time, creating challenges for management and for advisers in remaining competitive during a period of significant regulatory upheaval. Personally, this gave me the advantage of seeing the many sides of financial services regulation, before growing up with the ever-increasing compliance burden. This was an advantage because it allowed me to begin my compliance understanding from its outset, rather than being thrown in at the deep end some years down the line. I am grateful for this early understanding of both rules and ethics of the regulatory requirements.

Rules and compliance for any business are there for the protection of the end consumer. In addition, if good quality work and sales are being promoted it also offers strong protection for the business offering the sale and its adviser or salesperson. Compliance is a good business practice rather than a chore and one that should be embraced at all points of the sale by both client and salesperson.

Before the changes in regulation in 1988, many businesses did not maintain robust sales processes. That includes the need for full client fact finds or Terms of Business. It raises the question of how could you know your client well enough to provide the correct advice? There was also limited regulation of the glossy retail brochures detailing performance figures from various insurance companies on their investment performance. Surely, 15 per cent return each year is reasonable for any high-charging policy? As time has shown, this is not the case.

Insurance companies and retail banks started to look at their retail distribution models and the ways that they could maintain and increase sales and volumes, in terms of both income and clients. Buying up estate agents and placing mortgage brokers in as many of the branches as possible allowed a convenient sales route selling the insurance products of one company that to some extent (bearing in mind the sales volumes at that time) was quite successful. However, it transpired that this business model required these inflated volumes *as the norm*. As the MIRAS bubble burst, the model was not sustainable the recession that followed from 1989-90 onwards. Having just settled into the mortgage advice role, more than six years worth of successful sales were to follow through the recession and out the other side.

The tax relief MIRAS came and went. Compliance and the new regulatory authorities came and stayed.

After training, a new junior mortgage broker was recruited to replace me and I was relocated within the Southern Region to start sales production at a new branch on the Surrey/Berkshire border. This was fortuitous because property values were high and so were the mortgages to buy them. The property business was still booming at that point, but was about to burst in the autumn of 1988 and into early 1989. Having established an office, I was to experience 18 months of hard grind before a senior mortgage broker resigned in another higher-volume office and the company needed to fill the gap quickly. The 'poison chalice' that was the most successful branch in the Southern Region was mine for the taking.

This was a great opportunity — however it's always worth remembering that even the rosiest looking promotion can have its thorns. It is possible that the previous incumbent fleeced the client bank for every penny just before you arrived, leaving a barren wasteland of what had once been a reasonable prospecting area. The positive aspects of these situations must be grasped as they offer valuable learning points that can be added to your arsenal in future times, especially if you decide to run your own business. You will have certainly learned how to generate business from a tricky start point as a minimum.

One of my colleagues in Sussex at the time had become an 'industry hack' and was a true professional at his role. Tim, a rather dapper chap in his early forties, talked to me about the benefits of staying physically fit (he ran twice a week and visited the gym as often as work would allow) in a sales role, believing that keeping the body as well as the mind agile was highly beneficial. I have to admit to suffering from a waistline that likes to put-on a few extra inches — but I do what I can to keep the right side of fit. And I believe this also reflects on your client's perception of whether you care about yourself and your own wellbeing, as well as about his or her finances.

Some of my clients have employed me specifically because they know I will outlive them and be around to pick up the pieces for the family after they are gone. That's fine by me, but keeping fit helps.

I learned my profession well and moved around various estate agent offices as a tied representative, selling mortgages and the relevant policies of one company as an addition to the loan agreement. There were no procreation fees from mortgage lenders at that time as there are now; it was simply insurance policy sales that counted towards your sales target.

Mortgage leads were generated from the offices of the estate agent applicants. Many hours of tepid if not cold calling followed each week, to get appointments and the subsequent conversion to sales, as required by the sales director. The cold calling was so intense that after many years of doing it I have acute hearing in one ear, my telephone ear, and little hearing at all in the other. If you go into a sales role then you'd better learn to enjoy the telephone and client interaction on it. This will take practice and listening carefully to reactions and changes in tone to achieve success. It will pay dividends if you are an adept telephone user.

A note about technology in our profession, and to add some perspective to this time: I got my own personal mobile phone around 1991. Margaret Thatcher left office at the end of 1990 and the first Gulf War in Iraq ended around the same time (February 1991). Bryan Adams was about to rule the charts for 16 weeks with *(Everything I Do) I Do it for You*, the Robin Hood theme song.

Having a mobile phone was a real first for many people, and my employer enjoyed being able to get hold of me more easily, even though they would not pay a bean towards its cost. This was the first of a generation in our office and the phone used GSM technology, whatever that is. Everyone had seen the mobile phone 'brick' that had gone before — you remember, the ones that looked more like a car battery than a phone.

But the new GSM technology was entirely new; a lot smaller and neater and, might I add, rather average to use. The first GSM typed SMS text would not be sent until two years later in 1993. The mobile technology advances in the last two decades, and improvements and the ability to use it to sell, have been meteoric.

What next for technology, within sales and financial services? Its applications are limited only by the inventor's imagination. We all need to think about the processes and objectives of the work we undertake, and see whether something more efficient can be achieved for the industry by looking at things in a different way.

Other than by mistake, this is the only way that the boundaries of our world will expand.

Technology was a blessing for allowing me to phone in my order to the take away when getting home from a late mortgage appointment. The fish and chips always tasted that bit sweeter at 9.30 in the evening if I had a signed life assurance proposal in your bag, although this was not good for my long term health. The reality of this evening sales life was that it played havoc on my social and home life, seeing the girlfriend if and when I could. In the early years this was not a problem, but as I got older and started to focus on what was important to me and my partner, the fun and to some extent the desire to sell mortgages began to wane.

Chapter 6 in a nutshell

Embrace legislative change and regulation; it will not stand still. It is good practice and will serve to protect both your clients and your own business.

The use of the telephone is an art, which needs to be nurtured to gain appointments, the start of the sales process. If you are not sitting in front of someone you are unlikely to sell anything.

7. Stand & Deliver

No, not the tune by Adam & the Ants, although it was good, but a reference to your objective to deliver your sales target.

In a sales process, some management pressure to achieve your sales targets is always worthwhile, as long as it is well focused. Sales targets are a strange beast at the best of times, but targets are your guide to how you are expected to deliver your performance. Do you stop selling if you exceed your target expectations? *No!*

I was promoted and became an area manager for the region. Has anyone else noticed that accepting promotion usually means a higher level of work, with far greater responsibility, for less reward? When your P60 for the last three years shows a reduction in income of £200 each year and inflation is on the rise, then alarm bells start to ring — especially when you were not talking about much income in the first place. Your job title very quickly becomes *Regional Mug*, rather than the more impressive sounding official title of the role you took on.

Now who was in the wrong here? The answer has to be *me*. But why?

I had not clearly understood the gravity of the new role and had not negotiated very well. More fool me — but again, these are valuable learning points that I used in future career negotiations.

There are times when some managers rather miss the point of selling, preferring only to study sales data to improve their team's performance. The data they study are usually Key Performance Indicators (KPIs), which in the hands of an experienced individual can be highly valuable.

Personally, I don't have a problem with KPIs; in fact, with intelligence applied to the data, KPIs can be very helpful in guiding the process of improving sales performance. The problem word here is *intelligence* when applied to some middle managers. The two phrases may not go together, as I am sure you are aware.

Taking management information a stage further, I worked for one company who had a highly sophisticated KPI system that monitored everything you undertook in the sales process. Examples were conversion of first appointments to second appointment, sales achieved, product sales per meeting, sales across the product range, etcetera . . . you get the picture.

All individual section results were colour-coded red, green or blue, almost like a traffic-light system. Each screen had thirty or more aspects of the adviser's achievements displayed. When you walked into your sales manager's office for your monthly debrief, you could squint at the screen and if overall it was green or blue then it was going to be a reasonable meeting. However, if it looked like a bloodbath when your eyes squinted then it was worth keeping them that way as it was likely to turn into a bloodbath before the end of your meeting and you might want to consider your career options. Happy days!

The production and sales figures were put on the notice board for all to enjoy. Anyone caught being too much of a goody-goody by the troops was given a good ribbing on a regular basis. Office rapport at its best!

The reality of this process-driven style of management and its effects on sales force recipients is that many people either do not like being managed in this way, or are unable to extract the benefit of the information being provided.

Talking of *management guidance*, my sales manager often guided me away from offering split mortgages. How did a split mortgage work? An example was to offer advice and sales on a mortgage of £30,000 on an interest-only basis backed by an endowment to take full advantage of the MIRAS situation detailed earlier, and the balance of the mortgage on repayment, backed by a life assurance policy. If the prospect client was over 40, especially a smoker, the commission from the life assurance policy was greater than the commission on an endowment, especially in the early 1990s as you will see shortly. You were also selling two policies and it was better overall advice for the client. In addition, during the sales process the client got a comparison of endowment and repayment mortgages to give a balanced view (more on this point later!), which, all in all, was a very ethical sale.

Not according to my sales manager. '*No!* Sell endowments,' was the order. 'They pay more commission!' However, understanding your sales manager and your sales process is the key to controlling the correct and successful outcomes of your work, irrespective of the profession or industry you work in.

I want to break free

At the end of 1991, Freddie Mercury of Queen fame died. The day before he died, Freddie declared that he had suffered from HIV/AIDs for many years, although speculation had been widespread for some time. Why am I mentioning this? In my opinion, he was the first really famous person of a generation to die from the effects of this disease, and the significance of HIV/AIDS was starting to be noticed in the insurance profession.

The release of the Queen single *The Show Must Go On* in October 1991 became more poignant after his death just six weeks later.

AIDS was officially identified in 1981 and given its title in July 1982, although it can be dated back to the 1960s. It was only in the mid to late 1980s that the true catastrophic potential of this syndrome became apparent. Up to 2008 it is estimated that around 25 million deaths had been recorded globally but the full extent of the anticipated threat in the UK has not currently been realised.

Some publications were writing that 'no one is safe from AIDS', and many insurance actuaries began to increase life assurance rates to cover the potential for increased claims (and as a consequence increasing the commissions payable). It took many years for life assurance rates to reduce — but they did fall over time.

A further consequence of this situation is that many single-life assurance applicants, usually male, are currently required to undertake an AIDS test in the medical underwriting process.

It's your target, take pride in it

Do you remember my first comments about a relative sitting in front of you, and asking them to sign the application form? Do what is right for the client, not what meets someone else's sales targets. You represent the advice you provide, both now and into the future.

When you are planning ahead for the next few months' business, you will normally build a pipeline of potential sales. I have come to think of this as the *sausage machine*. Why? You feed ingredients into one end of the machine in order to have sausages coming out the other.

The chances are that, once you have established your sales production, you will work on a *thirds basis* to keep this production flowing as follows:

1. Creating new business, one third of your time

2. Signing up proposals and administrating sales, one third of your time

3. Completion of sales, one third of your time

It is vital that all three bases in your *sausage machine* of sales production are working at the same time, like spinning plates, to ensure that one area does not become idle at any given time.

When it comes to forecasting your sales output, with a little experience you will know exactly which client is going to do what business at what time within your machine. You should not waste much time with prospects or enquirers that, after some investigation and qualification, are never likely to lead to a good quality compliant sale.

You will know which sales are realistically going to complete that month and when that is likely to pay and put money in the bank. Remember that *gut feeling I wrote about earlier?* Make your stand and deliver as you know it will happen.

With a good and practised system in place, when your sales manager asks you how much you are going to sell this month, you can give him the real sales figure to the £1, although this may not be the figure that he wants to hear. However, if he is a good manager he will work with you to understand your reasoning to reach the same conclusion, or probe any shortfall in your expectations. This should be teamwork at its best.

It is better to be straight and transparent than to flannel over a situation, especially if your bonus is at stake. Bluffing about a monthly forecast only gives you around thirty days at the most to dig yourself out of the hole that you have just created by being over-optimistic.

How will you enjoy it?

What do you like doing best? And do you do this regularly if work allows? If you work hard then make sure you play hard. Enjoy reaching your target, it's one of the easiest ways that I know to excel further, either by buying everyone a drink in the pub after work or doing your own thing. Celebrate your success and that of those around you, even if you didn't quite make it this week or month. Support them as they will support you.

For me, a good week was being at home at 4.00 pm on a Friday afternoon putting stripes on my lawn in preparation for a weekend of sun worshipping, whilst puffing a freshly cut large Cuban cigar which would last most of the weekend. It was like a lawnmower being pushed by a large plume of smoke. But on a cooling summer's afternoon, it could not be beaten. And talking of lawnmowers....

Chapter 7 in a nutshell

Although the offer of promotion is a great personal compliment, don't jump at it without checking what's on the other side. Negotiate where you can, but take the opportunities when they arrive.

Understand your managers. Get to know how to control them using the compliance system they apply to help you.

With sales projections, tell your manager what you believe is achievable, not what they want to hear. It will repay you in the long run and create trust between you and the team. Under-offer and over-deliver!

Sign here, here and here!...

8. The lawnmower complaint

You are always responsible for the financial advice you provide. Let me give you an example of how this can come back to haunt you years later in the form of endowment complaints. You might like to think of these as *lawnmower complaints*. Here's why.

Let's imagine George is mowing his lawn with his shiny new lawnmower. Bob, his neighbour, leans over the fence to covet George's new acquisition and admire his neat lawn.

With envy written across his face he enquires: 'Going up in the world George?' gawping at the mown lawn with its precise stripes.

'Morning, Bob. No, I made a complaint about the mortgage endowment that I bought years ago and they sent me a cheque. They were all talking about it at the pub. Have you got an endowment, Bob?'

'Yes, two plans actually, but I never really understood either of them, Was I meant to?' says Bob excitedly.

'Tell you what, Bob: when I have finished cutting the lawn, I will drop you round a copy of the complaint letter that I got off the Internet. If you take a copy and send it off to your endowment companies, they should send you a cheque. There's a good deal on lawnmowers at the moment,' he adds with a grin.

'Sorry George, isn't that wrong?'

'Well, um, no! Everyone's doing it and if they are giving away free money, you may as well have your share. It gets you a new lawnmower!'

'OK, great! See you shortly George. Nice stripes on the lawn by the way.'

Many of the insurance companies did not keep records of endowment sales after a few years, simply because they were not required to. Starting around 2000, there was a campaign by some publications encouraging those affected to make complaints about the 'mis-selling' of endowment policies in previous years. Possibly encouraged by the potential for a new lawnmower as an example, many consumers took to their computers to take advantage of this situation, even though in some cases they did not actually believe they had been mis-sold anything. The complaints came in thick and fast.

If you were still a Regulated Individual (known as an RI), as all advisers who stay in the industry should be, the complaint could even, as a last resort, be forwarded to your home address because the insurance company of which you used to be a tied agent and employed by did not keep any records of the sale — although they had managed to keep your contact details on file. But *you* remained responsible for the advice, and there were few options available to the insurance company other than to ask you to remember what went on.

Strictly speaking, personal contact details should have remained confidential under the Data Protection Act. However, I know of many cases where an insurance company would access its own database to provide the former adviser's current home address (even more than ten years after the policy was sold) and send him or her the complaint at home to answer, accompanied with a letter explaining the adviser's responsibilities and the potential consequences of not responding.

One insurance company I know of had subsequently changed structure in a corporate merger and was unable to locate all its client records. I believe that some consumer groups got wind of similar situations thus exposing the potential limitations of insurance company processes. It could be suggested that *no records* means *no defence* and the complaint begins to gain traction within the objectives of the complaint guidelines.

You might argue that this is a 'guilty until proven innocent' approach to regulation — and that would not be far from the truth. However, it is also true that if the companies had paid greater attention to their records for longer, they would not have had to refer for information to former employees who had in many cases merely been toeing the corporate line.

When this happened to me, I phoned the insurance company to ask what was going on, as the covering letter was bordering on threatening. The responses to the questions I posed on the telephone were interesting:

'You think this is bad? You should see the other company [that had merged within the group]. We have no records at all!' explained the administrator.

'So what happens if you have no records and can't get any recollection from the adviser in the case concerned?' I probed.

'Oh, if that happens we pay some compensation and close the case,' said the voice dismissively. Very reassuring!

Do you remember the trouble I explained before, with selling split mortgages: one part being endowment and the other part a repayment basis? It was time for me to prove that this was the right advice and these endowment complaint responses gave me an opportunity.

Examples of comments and responses:

- 'I was never offered a repayment option.'

  Response: Even though you have a split endowment/ repayment loan.

- 'I did not know that the policy was investment backed.'

  Response: Even though you have had ten years of annual bonus statements.

- 'No comparison of repayment/endowment benefits was offered.'

  Response: Even though each computer generated illustration provided as part of my standard sales process had both endowment and repayment illustrated side by side to compare costs.

For those who were genuinely mis-sold by some unscrupulous soul, I wish the claim system had been easier and quicker for you. Those who made mis-selling claims under incorrect circumstances, I hope you enjoy sweet dreams after using your shiny new lawnmowers.

By 1993, time was running out for my career as a mortgage broker. I was getting bored and, more importantly, poorer by the year. Surely there must be more to life than this, I thought? It seemed to be a path leading to a dead end. The job had taught me that I enjoyed client contact. However, I had also learnt that I did not enjoy selling something, in this case mortgages, to make my living from the sale of an insurance on the back of the sale of the loan.

Industry exams were becoming the norm in order to meet compliance and business requirements, and continuing professional development (CPD) had become a regulatory requirement as the rules started to bite. I struggled with this process at first — but then I found the exams and reading interesting, especially as a way forward. It is sad to realise that among the things in life that I find interesting are insurance and pensions!

I had been successful at mortgage and insurance sales and had consistently met my targets throughout the 1990s recession but now it was time to move on. Selling pensions, investments and life or health insurance had to be a way to progress, and certainly a way of improving both my career prospects and my potential income.

As I alluded to before, the evening and Saturday morning mortgage sales meetings were beginning to wear on both my professional and personal life. I was 26 and beginning to settle down with a lady who became my first wife. My desire to be more stable the in hours of my work was growing. Snatching evenings with my partner subject to client meetings was becoming unacceptable to both me and her. Something had to give and the job was to go. As you will also discover, so did our marriage, eventually.

In an emergency, exits are located here, here and here!

Don't leave it too long before leaving a job, throwing a tantrum in the process that will keep the office gossips going for months.

Do yourself a favour and plan the exit early and carefully. Always be courteous and professional in your resignation process. This world we occupy is all too small and you never know when you will bump into someone from the past.

By deciding to move on, you have reached Base Camp One in deciding that you are, like Elvis, 'leaving the building' and that's the biggest hurdle to overcome. But what next? When was the last time you visited, reviewed and updated your CV? If it's not up to date then sort it out now. You need your CV out there doing your initial sales work for you. Be discreet and don't discuss it with your work colleagues at the pub after work or anywhere else. Information like that has a habit of slipping out at the wrong time.

Always secure your new post before resigning. Get your new offer in writing and accept it in writing before telling your old boss the good news. Your confidence in getting a new appointment can dissipate fast when you are out of work. And remember, however much of an idiot your manager is, be courteous.

The old boss may beg you to stay (and mine did offer a higher salary, which is not a motivator but a hygiene factor, which he would have known had he read Herzberg's motivation-hygiene theory). Stick to your *real* motivator, which is to move up. Be nice about it though, because you never know when your paths may cross again.

One autumn day in 1993, about lunchtime, I decided that I had had enough and my next reincarnation was on its way. The provision of insurance and pensions advice was my way forward and I secured employment as a sales representative in the South East for another life assurance company.

No mortgages to sell — I had promised myself I would never sell another one — but lots of financial planning qualifications to achieve and a big jump in salary.

No more weak cups of tea for me in darkest Reading at 7.00 pm, wondering which take away I could snatch a meal from before getting home to Guildford at 10.00 pm.

I had a break of one week between jobs and took my motorcycle test in Wimbledon over three days, rattling up the A3 at 7.00 am each day on a very tired 125 Honda commuter bike in the pouring rain. There's nothing like a challenge before starting another challenge. This employment was to start in the spring of 1994, around the same time that changes to our regulator were to occur with the introduction of the Personal Investment Authority.

This regulatory change also heralded the introduction of many other advice changes, such as greater transparency in detail of commission. Many feared this change at the time but it was another form of good governance to ensure that the consumer was fully informed of the contracts they were buying.

Why do people fear change? When I resigned, my employer argued that I was trying to avoid the impact of the regulatory changes by starting elsewhere and that if I thought it through properly I would decide to stay. In fact, it was good to be making a move at this point because it allowed me to learn the new regulatory processes within a framework of new products and the ethos of the new employer, without the burden of what had gone before.

On this note of past change, we can now look to the future with further significant changes being prepared for financial services. This constant upgrading of rules as understanding improves is the same in all industries. For UK retail financial services advice, the FSA plan to revisit the classifications of advice — independent, tied, etc — to restrict the advice levels available dependent on the business model, and also to specify the qualifications of client-facing advisers and salespersons.

This is a significant step, and some people are suggesting that the fallout from the profession could be equally great. However, in my opinion, there is also the risk that some consumers could be priced out of the advice market. These changes will need to be managed and other distribution models, such as the Internet, will have to be employed to maintain and extend market share.

In 1994, it was time for me to get on with my new career challenge.

Chapter 8 in a nutshell

Standardise the compliance elements of your own sales process. Make sure they are correct and don't deviate from them.

Keep personal notes of how you operated your business sales in case of future disputes. Whatever else you do, keep your records safe for future reference and your own protection.

Reinvent yourself regularly, embrace change or get out. You could get into a rut if you don't keep fresh.

Sign here, here and here!...

9. The objectives of TEF

TEF: Treating Everyone Fairly

For the record, I am very encouraged by the Financial Services Authority (FSA) initiative, running for a couple of years now, called *Treating Customers Fairly*, or 'TCF' for short.

This initiative is customer focused and ethically based. Its process requires transparency and prudence from companies offering financial advice and will only help our profession, placing the client at the heart of the process. This is good news for the overall image of financial services and the public we serve.

However, don't forget that you, the adviser, should also be treated fairly. I once heard a colleague say that a client will warm to a company that treats its staff *as well as* its clients fairly. If a company cannot treat its staff right, the customer (or *client*, my preferred term) does not stand a chance of a fair outcome — and I agree with this sentiment.

In my opinion, a *customer* buys once; a *client* wants an ongoing relationship and repeats business with you over time. This is a trust issue. I know how I prefer to think of them and which of the two I want to have in my own client bank. I would much rather deal with *clients* than *customers*.

When selling whatever product or service you offer, don't create a rod for your own back that you will almost certainly regret later. Clients need educating in the advice process too, because they care about their hard earned cash and they trust you to look after it for them. They have bought you and the service you offer.

If they ask you to see them in an evening or at a weekend, then that's what they will expect in the future. 'In the future' could be next month and next year and every year thereafter. If your client wants a home visit and you accept, then you will have little option but to revisit their home any other time they ask. If you protest, the riposte will be: 'Well, that's what you did last time!' followed by: 'I don't think it's necessary to see you at your office!' By this stage you will have lost some rapport and will already be on the back foot.

If you want to be treated as an equal, then start on an equal footing. This will not work for each client and you may need to bend the rules of engagement in some circumstances, but generally speaking the approach is sound.

Alarms bell should ring if you are asked to meet for a review or meeting at a pub or hotel outside normal working hours. This usually means that the enquirer sees the meeting as a social event, rather than a business meeting. You are there to work; they might be there for a free beer and a chat, with little or no intension of ever doing business with you. They wouldn't meet a solicitor or a doctor in a pub to discuss personal issues which could be overheard so why should they meet you there? Do you really want the barman to know your salary, date of birth, sexual preference and so on?

Personally, I'd rather spend evenings and weekends with family and friends than a business enquiry. Remember, you have a family or a partner or friends, a social life, hobbies and such like and they are important both now and into the future as your life develops and evolves. After two divorces, I speak from this experience. If this book ends up as a salutary lesson on how to get the work-life balance wrong, then my work as a marriage guidance counsellor is done.

Ah, divorce. There is more than enough 'meat' in this subject to fill the second *Churchouse Chronicles*. Divorce is a strange and hollow institution at the best of times, with the only winners usually being the legal profession at the end of the matter. However, in fairness, many solicitors are now making significant and positive steps to improve the situation with collaborative processes, such as mediation. I for one welcome these but sadly it is too late for me to use these initiatives.

The strains of the new job and its subsequent promotion took their toll and my first marriage was over a short time later. The lawn never looked the same again.

The playground values that will never leave you

Have you ever found yourself in a work or home life situation, where you think to yourself: Hello, are we back in the school playground now?

When I was of the age to run around a playground in Reading — playing football, getting involved in the odd fight and wandering how girls worked (not that you could ask your mates because that would be sissy!) — I never realised that certain experiences would follow me through life into adulthood.

As with any evolution, however, in the playground you are learning and beginning to understand who you really are and how you fit (or don't fit) into the hierarchy of society. In the playground that is Life, you find out who you are going to push around and who can thump you harder, who you like and who you don't, who you trust and who is going to pick you in the line out for the rugby team. (The thumping in this regard tends to get a bit harder as you get older.)

What you are learning are your own values, what matters to you. All of this learning will be different and personal to each of us. Take time to understand your own learning and the limits of your personal values. Just like in the playground, people will challenge the limits of these values as you go through life.

Make sure that you maintain the authenticity of your values and beliefs. Should you let people cross the 'fence' that is a value to you, and trample over what you hold true? My answer is a resounding *no!* These intrusions from others need to be controlled. To do that, you must know where your boundaries are as they will need protecting — and, to some extent, patrolling — to ensure that your borders are not breached.

You will refine these *borders* as you get older. Some will argue that as people get older they get more *grumpy* and that their personal borders or values extend out. There may be some truth in this.

Your clients will also teach you *their* values and borders and you may decide, as you evolve, to change your values to match those of other people. Clients, in their various different forms and types, will teach you many things and this is a perk of the job. Whoever's *borders* you might take on, you clearly respect them and their values. You have visited their borders and you understand them. Whatever you do, *know, understand and guard your values*, for they are yours and yours alone.

Think about these *borders*, your values, and treating yourself fairly, when your egotistical sales manager leans on you to meet your sales target by taking that late appointment (after the sales manager himself goes home!) with a couple who are 'ever so pleasant' but you know have no intention of signing up; then think again. You are not here to act as their evening's entertainment.

Focus on what you need to achieve (not a KPI target that ticks a box rather than actually achieving something positive) both for this month's target and in future years. A customer might meet a sales target; a *client* meets many years' worth of sales targets. The personal reward of the latter is far greater, in terms of both income and personal satisfaction.

Tied sales representative

The first part of my career in financial services sales was hard work but rewarding nevertheless. Some have pointed out that it was the springboard to my future.

My new role as a tied sales representative was a refreshing opportunity. Being 'tied' as a sales adviser to one product provider had not been an issue, although there are many people who would always contend that independent advice is always preferable. Arguably, independent financial advice offers greater flexibility in the offering that you provide to a client in your recommendations. That said, with a good in-house range this potential 'limitation' in provider range for products was not significant.

Starting with no industry qualifications, the summer of 1994 was spent revising the Financial Planning Certificate (FPC) exams 1, 2 and 3 and these were attained over the next 18 months, which allowed me to qualify as a financial adviser. Much time was spent poring over books whilst listening to Madonna's *Vogue* single. I have to admit to being stopped in my tracks by the death of Ayrton Senna, the racing driver. I undertook the Advanced FPC exams quickly afterwards. Aspiring as I did to higher stations in the management structure (stupid boy!) I believed that industry qualifications would be a requirement of the company and the industry. This is because financial services advice is an aspirational trade in terms of both understanding and income.

Training at its most intense

The training I received was second to none and I am grateful for this— although at the time there were those who called it not so much training as brainwashing.

Good quality sales training has reached a level of sophistication that creates in the individual the professionalism necessary to achieve success. From your training, you structured your sales diary to improve productivity, which was worthwhile. Client sales meetings were booked on a Monday morning through to mid afternoon (if possible) to avoid the office gossip and chit-chat after the weekend. Telephone sessions were organised for a Tuesday morning because the likelihood of getting hold of people was higher at that time. An office meeting was regularly booked for an hour on a Wednesday morning to brainstorm the latest product or sales idea, then you went back to client-facing meetings. Again, sales meetings would be on a Thursday all day and if you got it right, administration on Friday and any follow-up phone calls would clear the decks for the weekend.

This was a focused and driven organisation and sales went well in terms of volume, value and diversity. However, always remember that you represent yourself first and *then* your company. No matter how good the product that you are selling, if the client does not buy you (your character, your values) then he or she is unlikely to buy your product, leaving you struggling for both sales volume and quality. And if you want your prospect as a *client* rather than a customer, then you want him or her to buy both now, and again in years to come.

It comes back to this: if the sales prospect were a family member, would you still make the sale?

Some organisations mechanised the process of building initial rapport with a prospect, to ensure that any recruit who struggled on the personality front could at least try to build a relationship with a client before fumbling through the rest of the sale. This was done by ensuring that any initial 'contact' questions at the beginning of the meeting were in the format of asking the prospective client about his or her past, present and future. This was very helpful to those less gregarious sorts who found small-talk difficult.

Taking this further, don't talk about yesterday's weather and today's weather and then next week's weather. It is not interesting and it never was! Your client's time is as valuable as yours; if they have given you the courtesy of an audience, then meet their expectation of *results*. Anyone who opens a sales meeting with a discussion about the weather needs to be put away.

Another training technique, designed to flatter clients, was *mirroring*, although it's one I don't use.

Mirroring means mimicking a client's movements. Done well, this can mean that the client sees someone like himself and people tend to like that. You could argue that a client is buying a reflection of himself, someone he can trust with his hard earned cash. Mirroring can be done in various ways, both visually and in your verbal communication. You can mimic by *tone*, speaking calmly when they do, and louder in volume when they do, to reflect a comment or statement. Done badly, however, it can look as though you are taking the rise out of the client; if you want the sale this should be avoided.

People like to talk about their favourite subject. Their favourite subject is usually themselves. Even if it is not, then it's still a good place to start because they will guide you from there to the subject they do prefer. And remember, they will not want to hear about your last illness or cold or the fact that you have a bad back or can't find the right childminder. These things are important to you, but to you alone.

If your prospect has a lovely house or garden, talk to him about it: 'What a great place! How long have you been here?' 'Wow! Look at your garden, that's fantastic! How long does it take you to look after?' These are all the usual 'open' questions that you should be using anyway but they are clearly focused *on the client*. It is a subject that they will have known about all their lives and a client is usually itching to tell you what they have been doing or what their plans are. So, ask the right questions and find out all about them.

As you prepare your sales approach, you will need to target your prospects to ensure that they offer you the opportunity for a sales conversion. Time and experience will teach you what signs and traits to look out for, such as home postcode, age and occupation. Each segment of society is different and needs to be approached differently to achieve sales success.

A good example is what type of cheque book you as the salesperson are trying to open to take a premium and make a sale. What do I mean by this?

Is it a personal contract or a business product that you are offering? In my experience, the attitude of directors and senior managers to opening the company cheque book in comparison to their personal cheque book can be very different. The company cheque book or company account seems to be an easier sale than that of a *personal* decision process and sale. There is no obvious explanation to this, other than that there seems to be some disconnection in the individual's decision process between company funds and personal money.

To make a point of this, I wish someone would explain to me the profession's fascination with the term *High Net Worth* (HNW) client. It's a term that creates much discussion, and it is something for which I am still trying to find a realistic definition. If a client has a need and is prepared to cover the fees proposed to provide a service to meet that need, does that mean you should not deal with them? If they don't meet an earnings criterion or don't have £1 million in cash available for instant investment, do you say: 'Sorry, I can't help you. Go and see the bank!' Of course not. Be profitable, be commercial and *do what is right for the client.*

We are all individuals and so are our clients. Make your own judgement and go with it; you know what you are looking for. If you are concerned that you may get tied up with little remuneration to show for your work, then put your fees up across the board and promote these to ensure that you attract the right type of enquiry and income. It's up to both you and the client to control the sales situation if you are going to have mutual respect in the future.

I once heard that a client relationship can be referred to as an emotional bank account. Just like most bank accounts: you can be in credit or debit. If you build the sales correctly, then by the time you get to closing the sale you should have a sufficient *credit* balance to make a withdrawal — in other words, to close the sale.

If you have not achieved a good sales approach, then the closing of a sale may mean that you have not enough *credit* to achieve success. Know where you are in the sale, to know what your balance is in the relationship and your client's emotional bank account.

This might sound a bit farfetched, but think about the sale you are working on now. Any salesperson will know which one they want to come in to meet their target. Are you in credit or debit right now? And if you could independently ask the client the same question, what would their answer be?

A role in sales will take you to many places that you would never visit otherwise, both physically and mentally, because a client's perception on life is invariably different to yours, as you will see in the next chapter. Enjoy the lessons that your clients will teach you.

Chapter 9 in a nutshell

Sell yourself first, then your product. In the sales process, people buy likeminded people and what products can do for them personally, not based on a rational assessment of product features alone.

Turn every sales enquiry into a policyholder.

Once a client has bought once, you can always revisit him to buy again.

Understand where you are in the sales process. You need to know whether you have enough credit in the relationship account to make the withdrawal – in other words, to close the sale. Rapport may come easily but it can also disappear quickly.

Sign here, here and here!...

10. Ducks, lakes and troubled waters

I received an enquiry from a new prospect and subsequently followed this up with a phone call and a meeting. Arriving at the business park in Sussex and locating his office, I arrived exactly on time (never keep them waiting!). I was met by a rather austere receptionist whose disgruntled attitude changed as soon as I mentioned the prospect's name . . .'Yes sir, certainly sir, I will get him for you shortly sir, coffee sir? Take a seat sir,' . . .as her interest in my attendance took a remarkable leap forward.

The owner of this particular technology company strode across the office and welcomed me with a smile.

'Keith, Gerald, welcome,' gushed our potential client, thrusting out his hand. He seemed a delightful, if rather rotund, man.

'Good morning, Gerald,' I replied as boldly as I could manage.

Gerald strode back to his office with me following in his wake. I noticed how every member of the junior staff suddenly looked very busy as he passed. On entering his vast and well-appointed office, he sat at a large glass desk. That desk was like an island in the ocean of the vast workspace. I fancied I could hear an echo with every word we exchanged, only partly absorbed by the expensive blue Wilton carpet that cloaked the floor.

At that point in my early career I was an eager young puppy dog representative (complete with wagging tail, wet nose and prepared to run after any sale even if it were utterly pointless) and had only just finished my rigorous training. This training consisted of drumming in the normal process of how to control a client meeting with the initial introduction— getting to know the client by building rapport — leading on to the client's attention, interest, conviction to proceed, and then the close for the business.

This meeting, however, did not go according to my 'training land' plan. I introduced myself and then set out a meeting agenda for both the client and me to follow, finishing with the close of the agenda with the words I had learned by rote.

'Is there anything else that you would like to cover in this meeting?' I asked, keen to recruit Gerald into the sales process.

He leaned across the desk and said with a smile: 'So, you don't want the business then!'

I paused. 'Or… we can do it your way!' I replied, uncertainly.

Gerald smiled (he had gained control) and we went on to *his* agenda. Many sales managers would say that this was just an *order take* rather than a sale, and to some extent they would be correct.

I took down Gerald's details and probed the other assets available. His deposit savings position was significant. Of course I had been trained not to be obvious about my natural interest in the possibilities of an extra large sale, and had always been advised to breeze past the opportunity — but then to collect sales hooks later in the questioning to allow me to revert back to this area at my leisure. However, on this occasion I was lost without directions and no hooks had been uncovered, so I went for the sale anyway.

'So, what are you going to do with the savings then?' I blurted, in a vain attempt to grab a sale.

'I'm going to buy a house!' was his smooth reply. Gerald already had a large house, so why he needed another was beyond me.

'Why?' I fumbled.

'Because my wife wants a lake,' he smiled.

Bemused, I enquired further: 'Why?'

'Because she wants ducks on it,' he laughed.

'And will she get the lake?' I asked, finding his laughter infectious.

'Oh yes,' he stated. 'Got to keep the wife happy!'

I was stumped, and amused, but went for the sales 'punt' anyway. I had nothing to lose. I asked if I could make a recommendation for some of the savings and he suggested I send him some details and he would think about it. So I did and he went ahead with a significant investment.

Here's the strange thing. Did I get into trouble for that sale? Oh yes! I had followed the full sales process but not the company procedure of referring the case to a senior staff member who would normally have handled larger-sized cases.

I can 'punt' for a sale as much as the next man, as you can see; no talent required.

Even with a flea in my ear, it was a satisfying outcome. I had got them a client in a compliant fashion — and I had done the right thing by the client himself, too.

As a note here, do you remember my comment in the opening chapter about 'The Bluffers Guide to Flogging Policies'? The first chapter in a book like this might be headed 'Punting'. Go easy on its use because it has very limited success, as will your career if you use it too often.

Our first moment together

I have said on many occasions that you represent yourself first and *then* the business that you work for. That is what a recruitment process buys: *you!*

As a professional, do you meet your client in a shirt, tie and a well fitting jacket? If it is hot, do you simply ask if you may remove your jacket rather than assuming that this is acceptable? You might call this a ridiculous suggestion — but there are older clients who consider this important etiquette, so give them the courtesy of asking.

And what about the first handshake with a new sales prospect? A handshake can send a very powerful message to its recipients. If you are shaking a man's hand, is your grip firm? And do you lighten this grip if you are shaking the hand of a woman? Is your eye contact good? Did you smile when you gave your greeting? Did you get up to greet your prospect or move across the room to give the client the warm welcome that they deserve, especially if you were expecting a sale at the end of the meeting?

If you answer *no* to any of these questions, and you ever wonder why you did not clinch a deal, then have a look at your initial contact as the first point of improvement. And remember, if the person you are greeting is attractive, do keep your eye contact in the appropriate places. As an example, my wife, Esther, grumbles about men who tend to greet her breasts rather than her face. Anyone doing this by her is given little regard.

Is the client meeting not the same scenario as applying for a job and turning up for an interview? If you were applying to be a stockbroker would you not attend an interview in a suit? And if you were applying to undertake manual work, wouldn't you ensure that you did *not* turn up in a suit? All these points are relevant at the point of the sale of 'you' in the interview process.

I was once told that a good car salesman will not approach a prospect in a showroom until they have touched a car. This is because the effort they are taking to touch a car is the signal that this model is what they are looking for, the first buying sign and an indication of their intent.

The same occurs for new or second hand cars, although some bangers with sunroofs and two exhausts are marketed as 'wheelbarrows'. Don't you just love the old jokes? The same principle can be argued with a handshake and your first approach in the 'showroom' that is your office or even their front room. Don't forget that there are usually two handshakes in any meeting: one at the beginning and one at the end. Both count, either to say 'I want the business please' or to say 'thank you for your time and your business'.

Both handshakes seal the deal, so ensure that both handshakes send the right message to your client, irrespective of who he or she is. Your personal sales standards should never fall, whether you are selling to a millionaire or to a low-income individual. They all matter.

I also once experienced a view from a highly successful salesperson who, at the point of a handshake, would also touch a client's elbow — almost a double touch. This shows warmth, but also breaks down further barriers. Now, please don't start touching clients anywhere you fancy. However, you could try this on a friend or family member and see whether you get a different and better reaction.

I might add that you may well fail without a good smile and the all-important eye contact. Don't forget to clean your teeth please!

Do you think that this principle of first contact could be extended to the telephone? You have heard of cheesy phrases, such as 'smiling on the telephone', but don't ignore this kind of advice. Whatever you do, whatever your style, be clear and concise in your sales telephone message and your offering whenever you talk to an enquirer or prospect. The message you provide them on the telephone should be replicated when you meet them face-to-face, otherwise you are likely to find yourself on the back foot straight away. Know your message off by heart and think about any tentative objections you might receive in securing an appointment. Overcoming objections is what your role is about, and this starts with making appointments.

Why do those irritating automated phone messages make people think that they will succeed in getting client contact? Maybe I should try it, 'Hi, I'm Keith, do you have a problem with your pension planning? Press 1 to solve this, 2 to become increasingly annoyed or 3 to be plunged into an abyss.' When will they learn?

Talking of being on the back foot, make sure that the person you are talking to is the decision maker. If not, what part will they play in the process of securing the sale you propose? Are they part of a decision team or only a conduit to get to the decision maker?

There is nothing worse than meeting a prospect to find out that the issue you are discussing is not really *their department* and needs to be passed up to 'Jennifer, who is head of procurement' or discovering that the decision maker in a household is not the spouse you are meeting.

At the first client meeting at your office, or on the client's first visit to your website, does this experience reflect your values and that of your sales process? If not, then resolving the discrepancy has to be high on your priority list.

Prospects will judge you on their first contact and form their initial thoughts at that point. Was the office or website clean and efficient? Was your desk piled high with paper or clean, approachable, functional and looking ready for business? Did you seat the client directly opposite you in a confrontational style, or are your meeting tables round and you sit *with* the client to create a friendly and approachable setting?

All of these issues count toward the overall perception of whether a client or enquirer can do business with you now and into the future. Remember, you want them as a *client* rather than a customer who buys once and then never comes back.

The next time you enter your office or look at your website, ask yourself a few questions. *Would I buy from these people*, seems an obvious place to start, doesn't it? But that's down to technique, really. No, I think the following are better questions to ask yourself:

• *Am I comfortable here?*

• *Is this a place I like?*

If you do not feel comfortable there and you don't like the place either then stop wasting time on your sales technique for the moment, because that message, the all important first sales impression, will be lost by the environment in which you operate.

Look at the decor of your office: the carpet; the cleaning; even the polish on your shoes. If you can't be bothered to get these right, then your prospects may not be bothered to do business with you. Don't wait to find out that this is the reason why you are not converting enquirers and prospects at the rate you always anticipated. If you are the business owner then this paragraph will be highly relevant. However, if you are a salesperson, then think about your environment and influence the business decision makers to make any necessary changes.

Whatever you do, don't spend the annual bonus on *tarting up* the office. Instead, make sure it represents you and your offering as it is your showroom. Above all, it has to mirror the aspirations of your prospects. You might disagree with me on this point but I can tell you from experience that it does work.

Chapter 10 in a nutshell

Always be prepared to adjust your process to reach the client concerned - although you will need to listen to their needs first.

Know your message off by heart and be confident and concise with your sales offering. Never apologise for making the client contact. You are proud of what you offer.

Understand the decision making process of a sale. Ensure that you are sitting in front of the person who can agree to the deal and sign the forms.

Sign here, here and here!...

11. You got promoted, stupid boy!

Employment promotion

Do you remember my comments about the potential disadvantages of promotion? Well, this promotion was no different. My naivety got the better of me again, and once I'd moved the surprise of the different attitudes of the two locations was a learning experience. All changes are opportunities to learn and different management styles can create new dynamics that need to be observed, enjoyed and to some extent controlled. A good manager can teach you well, however you may find that greater learning and depth of understanding can be gained from greater challenges presented by others.

The year was 1997 and I was maturing in my business prowess as I grew to understand and love the profession I had chosen. I had been successful in my role and it was time for me to take on the next challenge. The summer had been warm, the lawn was looking good and there is only so many times you can see *The Men in Black* whilst humming the theme tune by Will Smith before you have to look for other entertainment.

Not dressing the part?

To win promotion, we were required to attend a two-day and night evaluation with a group of other hopefuls and our respective regional directors in the Midlands. Having arrived at a plush hotel venue, the process started with a dinner, which led to two days of intensive testing. This may sound grim but in fact it was great fun!

After lunch on the first day, a test was prepared as part of our evaluation. We were required to pull a subject out of a hat and prepare a ten-minute presentation to all of the directors present. I was praying that my presentation subject would not be the pre-1987 pension rules for company pension plans. My trembling hand exited the black bowler hat and I read out my topic:

Class C drugs [as they were then] such as cannabis and marijuana should be legalised. Discuss.

As it happens, having been in the comprehensive system with a large teenage social network in an affluent part of the South East in my youth, I was not unaware of what substance was in what class and why. As a mature teenager I had even tried cannabis once — but it did nothing for me and I'd stuck with my 20 Marlboro a day, which I much preferred at the time.

A good way of telling if your presentation is going a bit too well, is when the directors have to stop you after 15 minutes and remark: 'You seem to know an awful lot about this, Keith?' with faces aghast.

It was time for me to shut up!

When you undertake presentations to an audience, whoever it may be, never underestimate the importance of controlling your breathing, especially at the start of your talk.

Consciously calm yourself. When standing for the first time (and you should always stand), lean forward and take a lengthy but controlled breath before smiling. With your first words, exhale gently, releasing the first part of your message in an authoritative manner. Try it, it works.

Pace yourself and your message and adjust both your tone and style to suit your audience. There is no hurry and your thoughts are important. The control and authority in the way you convey these will sell you *and* your offering.

You are not my granny and I don't want to teach you how to suck eggs — but here goes anyway: keep your hands out of your pockets during your presentation and remove any keys or loose change from your pockets before you start as these will jangle and distract the audience. Go to the toilet before your allotted time begins, to make sure that you don't shuffle around unnecessarily. Avoid pre-seminar drinks. There will be plenty for you afterwards if you want.

Portly gentleman

Two months after my promotion, I was informed at another meeting with my director that the career progress I craved was mine. He had a few guiding words for me in addition.

'One point that was noted during the assessment is that you are a portly gentleman and are not dressing correctly,' he stated. 'I would suggest that you see a tailor in accepting this offer and he will make you a double fluted, single breasted suit, dark of course. I would recommend you keep the outside pockets stitched up to ensure you cannot put keys in your pockets as this will bulk out the side shape, and I would suggest turn-ups.'

What could I do? My days of wearing M&S suits were numbered.

The irony was, that after spending £800 on two bespoke suits (this was 1997), I managed to rip both of them by accident within a fortnight. I was not a happy man.

Sometime later, we were due a quarterly branch inspection from this gentleman. Being a stickler for presentation, I had made sure that mine was in impeccable order. Pressed suit, polished shoes and washed car were all present and correct. I had a new enquiry meeting that morning and I would be back at the branch by midday.

The new enquirer was a brick manufacturer and, as I arrived at his premises, production was in full swing. On opening the car door I looked down to see a carpet of sludge surrounding my car and shoes. What a nightmare! But as they say, 'where there muck, there's brass'. The emergency clear up on the way back, just in time for my branch inspection, was well worth getting the business.

The director was a good man and I had great respect for his sales ethics. But with the proliferation of computers, mobile phones and online communication, responding to emails and mobile phones was making the sales role increasingly sedentary. With less physical 'running around' it was bound to have a negative effect on my originally svelte silhouette.

By *silhouette*, I now mean *large outline*. Maybe I will ask about a double-breasted suit next time?

Learning more from all styles of management

It's a strange comment but true, if you know what to look for. Learning from other people's mistakes, and your own, is difficult to undertake but very worthwhile.

Sometimes you get to a stage in business where you ask yourself: *What would my manager do?* And head in the entirely opposite direction knowing that you will be right. This feels both strange and to some extent amazing. A lesson in how *not* to achieve sales success followed in the forthcoming months.

One demonstration of inspiring commitment to sell was a concept called *Tune into WIIFM*. The acronym stood for What's In It For Me?

This came from a sales manager sharing a winning technique with his sales team. It was designed to explain that by putting more into the sales process you could get more out for yourself in terms of money and recognition. I think the phrase needed to be amended slightly to *What's In It For Him Only?*

Did this concept work? *No!* Did it breed contempt within the sales environment and team? *Yes!*

As part of the promotion of the company, a series of client seminars was organised each year to promote both the company and the branch staff to any invited prospects. A large, well-known venue in the locality was selected each time. This was partly to accommodate over 100 people in comfort, but also so that if the setting was a nice one, such as a racecourse or country club, then some attendees might come along just for the tea and cakes. It was run along similar lines to the AGMs of bigger PLCs and mutual organisations, and ensured that the venue was full and that the right client rears were on the right seats.

I had an experience where my manager fell ill just before a joint presentation at one such seminar. Although this meant my having to present his part as well as my own, with no time to prepare, it was an opportunity for me to shine rather than allow all our hard work to fall flat.

This sort of unexpected event always has a positive side to it. Surviving it, and even turning it into a personal triumph, means that any hiccup that ever arises at a public presentation is no longer a problem; you can overcome any issue to which you apply yourself and, as a theme throughout this book, if you always represent yourself first and foremost, you can excel.

Work that sales target, baby!

Your next task or promotion position is to *sell*. When you are given or have negotiated your sales target for the business or calendar year, how do you calculate how you're going to run your sales year?

It would *not* be intelligent to take your target, say £120,000 (for ease) income for the year, and divide it by 12 months (£10,000 per month) and then apply this to the year — would it? Please don't get the maths wrong at this point or you will never make a financial adviser. If you do that, you assume that you are not taking any holidays, that August and December will be as busy as the rest of the year, and that your production runs smoothly every month. Life and sales are not that easy.

You will have around six to eight weeks of holidays and short breaks during the year. If you don't take holidays, the likelihood is that you will burn out. Make sure you take breaks and get away from the business. I am sure the Blackberry will come with you anyway, so you won't be that far away from your beloved desk. But don't let the Blackberry (or your laptop) become the third party named in your divorce papers. A holiday is what it means and this is the time to give back to both yourself and your loved ones. Strawberry Dakaris on the sun-drenched beach in Barbados don't drink themselves you know. They need you!

Taking holidays and breaks out of your calendar should allow you to divide your business production year into ten months, and then think about the peaks of production in that year.

As an example, in financial services my experience has shown me that peak production comes twice a year, namely April-May and November. The first peak is usually attributable to the end of the Tax Year and the November peak is because most people love a deadline. What do I mean by this? With Christmas around the corner, they look at their finances, realise that they have not done the financial planning they promised themselves as a New Year's resolution eleven months before, and then want to get on with it.

To be successful you and your family should realise that you probably won't be having a holiday in those three months.

The months where you would not expect sales and production to be high could be December, January and July-August or 'holiday months and planning months' as they are otherwise known to you now.

Within these months, you should also be planning or updating your sales strategy to ensure peak performance in the other months, noted as April and November. Updating your sales strategy every quarter is worthwhile because sales seasons are like the actual seasons. And as you well know, in the UK they don't always work correctly.

By taking these thoughts into account, your sales target of £120,000 production for the calendar year might be divided as follows, as an example:

Month	Sales Target	Other Notes
January	£6,000	Planning month
February	£9,000	Building sales
March	£12,000	
Review your sales progress and strategy		
April	£16,000	Peak sales
May	£15,000	Peak sales
June	£10,000	

Again, review your sales progress and strategy

July	£ 8,000	Planning month
August	£ 6,000	Holiday and planning
September	£ 8,000	Building sales

*Last quarter, review and change
to meet your overall strategy*

October	£12,000	
November	£16,000	Peak sales
December	£ 7,000	Planning month and a bit of partying.
Total	£125,000	Your sales target + 5%

Please adjust these figures to meet your own ambitions and expectations.

Always put in a positive margin to your sales target to keep your manager happy and on side. Remember, you need to control him in the process, not the other way round.

Assuming you are good at what you do (and you are), you would expect to produce more than the average for the branch or the region. That is only fair. But *make sure you know what these averages are* to measure the true requirement that you are being asked to achieve. And if you don't agree, in the positive or negative sense, then make sure you stand your ground and negotiate hard. This will allow you to prepare your personal sales target in a more positive and aspiration light.

In addition, you may be able to bring other negotiating tools to your sales target meeting by offering to help your immediate group and your company as a whole. You might suggest that you add value by championing new ideas or helping other members of the team or new recruits on a 'buddy system' approach.

New ideas and initiatives are the lifeblood of any progressive organisation and they usually start at ground level. Always add to the party more than you take away, and ensure that the world you operate in improves on your watch. Push the barriers of production and innovation to make your organisation better than it was.

Sadly, the 1st January can be a de-motivating day when your good sales year clocks over to a nil figure to start the following year. Pull yourself (and probably your hangover from the party the night before) together and start planning again. However good the party was, and I have been to some excellent ones, the sales target will still be there and the bills will keep rolling in. The family will still support you and your objectives so get ready in yourself.

It's all very well discussing and planning for your sales *year* ahead. To achieve those goals you also have to plan for the *day* ahead. Some of the most successful people I have met are not the sharpest knives in the drawer — but they do have the ability to plan their future, whether that be the next hour, day, week or year.

Some success can be put down to something as simple as a *To Do* list every day. I have used this system and it works well. It allows you to extract more benefit from your working day. And the cost to you? A five-minute *brain dump* at the beginning of the day, to note what you need to do and achieve — irrespective of whether that task be large or small, complicated or simple — get your notes down on your list every morning. Then have a highlighter pen handy and strike each task through as you achieve the end of each item.

At the end of the day you should have a coloured piece of paper, sporting all those lines through the tasks proposed. If you fail to achieve a task then it goes to the top of the next day's *To Do* list. I also find that going for the hardest tasks first helps me — but again, that is partly because I am a morning person, and most of my productive energy happens early in the day.

Don't forget to add 'Go home at end of day!' at the bottom of your list to ensure that you achieve this.

Try it for one week and see whether your productivity and satisfaction levels increase. I think you will find it works.

Turn on the TV now, it's over

The end of the line came in December 2000 when the company I worked for closed to new business. It was a strange and sad day, and one that will stay with me forever. I felt that I had committed to this company. I had found my professional home. But the writing had been on the wall for months, and to some extent it came as no surprise. We all knew that something drastic had to happen to solve the accounting situation — but it was still a daunting proposition.

I was awakened by a phone call at 6.15 on a cold December morning.

'Turn the TV on now!' barked a rather urgent voice. The end of my current employment situation was on the television, as the smiling BBC presenter detailed how the demise of my beloved employer had arisen and what the prospects were for everyone involved.

Having dressed, I jumped in my BMW, a bronze orange coupé and no, I am not colour blind, grabbing some toast on the way, and promptly made my way to the office. The irony of Bob the Builder on his way to the Christmas number one singing *Can we Fix it?* over the car radio was not amusing. Clearly, in this case he couldn't!

In big business, I know there are protocols that need to be followed to tell regulators and government before any information is leaked to the public, and this usually means that the staff and the policy holders are told last. One day, maybe, the regulatory powers-that-be will look at this and resolve to improve the human aspect of this deeply unsatisfactory communication situation.

The following weeks were difficult for staff and policy holders alike, with many complaints being received by the organisation about its demise. The final days for the staff came in February 2001, around the time of the Foot and Mouth crisis. I don't think the two issues were related. At the time of finishing this book, the end for the policyholders was still not in sight.

A big motivational and retention session was held in a London hotel, to sell a new employment offer to the team to keep us together. What a jolly jape! Surely the managers were on a bonus offer within a corporate retention programme, to keep as much of their sales teams together as possible? Clearly the sales staff represented the chief value to the purchasing business. I have never seen a bunch of managers fawning over their staff so eagerly; it was all very undignified.

Brown envelopes were issued to all, good and bad containing the individual severance notices and the offer to start employment with another company — in the same building in the same role, at your usual desk with the same telephone...and of course your company BMW.

No! This was a very odd reality and one that was not attractive. It was time to leave the ship that had sadly run aground.

I am honoured to have had the experience of working for a stalwart of the insurance world and for that I have no regrets. Personally, I lost out — like many other policyholders — but then that can only be expected because of my personal belief in what I had been selling.

The ship sank. Much gnashing of teeth was to follow. At least it had funded a messy first divorce in the meantime.

Chapter 11 in a nutshell

Map out your sales year to give yourself space and thinking time to achieve success.

'Brain dump' what you need to achieve each day on to a To Do list every morning and watch your productivity increase. It's your list and you know what you want to target and achieve.

Represent yourself first, not what others want you to do, especially when the ship is sinking.

12. Double-edged swords

Benefits in kind can be a doubled edged sword

Your salary may be reasonable but the commission or bonus will make the difference — along with the company car and pension. When you have no doubts about your own abilities, then bonus payments should be regular and bountiful.

This raises a few questions. Will your anticipated bonus or commission actually be paid or does there in fact have to be a 'Z' in the month? The devil is in your employment contract detail.

The more complicated the commission or bonus structure, the more likely that your sales manager or director can arrange that it won't be paid. When they advertise 'on target earnings' of say £60,000 in a year, with a basic salary of say £30,000, they may really be saying that they will pay you £30,000 and pretend about the rest.

You won't stay in the role long if this proves to be the case. I have known many good people who have been screwed over by the sales organisation that they work for, with the employer hoping that the employee won't have the bottle to leave. Some of them don't and live to regret it.

Many companies will give you a training allowance alongside a basic salary. The training allowance is usually available for a period of say six months and makes the assumption that you will follow a standard training process such as:

- Becoming fully trained in the ways and culture of the company: two months

- Building a sales pipeline: two months

- Starting sales completions, with new sales also being built: two months

These are reasonable expectations. The purpose is that when the training allowance ends, then your resulting sales will provide the commission payments to make up for the allowance. Even better, if you get your sales going quickly, you could have significant income for an additional three months. All this is fantastic if it can be fulfilled by both parties to the contract.

This is not always the case. I have seen unfortunate situations where individuals get desperate over a particular sale being shared between two colleagues or two departments, even before the sale is made. Having suggested that we should 'get the sale first before arguing over who gets what' the argument has escalated to a level that almost makes the sale worthless because of the bitterness and wrangling that will greet its completion. Offering good client advice and completing a good sale should be a satisfying experience, not a disappointment.

My next point may seem obvious to anyone working in a sales environment. It has to do with the egos and hierarchy of a sales team or environment. It is of course the phallic symbol that is the company car.

One company I worked for used to produce a new car list every six months, showing which models the sales team could aspire to. The world would stop for most of that day as each individual compared and contrasted each car model with the options they could get, with a cap on an upgrade payment based on their grade in the company. I foolishly added money to a car selection once and regretted it. Even as a dedicated petrol head, I found this a bore and a waste of time.

Now, should I have the Audi with the optional leather or the Ford with the larger alloys? Decisions! Decisions!

I find it odd that some employers require you to put a mobile telephone number on your business card but decline to supply you with a phone. The purpose of the mobile number is to allow your clients to get hold of you — and also for your employer to be able to catch up with you, wherever *you* are.

However, there is a benefit to going along with this.

To improve your own prospects, always keep the same mobile number. Then, even if you do leave an employer, the *clients* can still contact you. Most employment contracts restrict you from contacting clients for a period of time after your employment and that is only fair. However, can this apply if the client is the one who contacts you? Remember, people buy people.

It's a team game

Most people like the sense of belonging, it provides them with ownership and bonds them to others who they may not otherwise know. It is the same in most groups, whether that be your cricket club or your sales team.

Let's turn to a different game – football.

What is it about financial services, that you must support or indeed worship a football team? You may have chosen to act the office swot and support the team that your company sponsors — but why is football so important? Is it part of the psychology of financial services?

It can be fun to watch an international game whilst sipping a cold beer but I wouldn't call myself a football fan. As I have matured I've grown out of my boyish interest in football, now preferring rugby and Formula One. I don't give a fig if Arsenal loses to Manchester United or the other way round.

However, whilst working in London I began to realise that this was not going to be acceptable to my colleagues. You *must* have a team. Denial is the straight road to social oblivion in the office.

So, Reading FC are my boys because I used to live in Reading. *There!* I have a football team and I instantly become part of the office '*team*'. I can hear you shouting already: 'Reading? They are rubbish!' Perhaps I made a poor choice of football team but, irrespective of your gender, *having no interest in football* is the thing that is totally unacceptable.

Luckily, you don't have to be interested to be able to bluff your way through. To keep myself sufficiently educated in these league matters, I would read the back page of the *Metro* newspaper on the daily commute. Then I could wind up my colleagues who supported whoever had lost the previous night's game, making some spurious remark about the fact that the second goal allowed was, in fact, offside and 'was the ref having a tea break when that went in?'

No one in the office need suspect that you neither know nor care about what really happened in the game or the league.

Strangely, however, if you ask your colleagues whether they think Jenson Button's soft tyre choice on his first pit stop was a wise move, bearing in mind the impending rain, you will be met with stony silence. Why does knowledge of one pointless activity work and not the other? That's one secret I simply can't fathom.

Talking of camaraderie, let me say a word about the value of quality colleagues — people you trust and respect, usually in the sales team that you work with. They might also be administrators working with the sales team.

As you mature, the football team may lose its importance and conversations will turn to families and their needs. Pay attention to this point, as it will bind the cohesion of your team.

Having a football team that you support is not important but being involved in the office banter most certainly is and should not be underestimated. *'Come on Reading!'*

The virtue of business life friends

As careers and employments change you meet lots of people in your everyday life. Some disappear as quickly as they arrive. Some you only *wish* would disappear as quickly as they arrive.

One or two true friends will hold your attention and friendship for years. Through hardship and glory, you will share professional wisdom for the benefit of both the industry and each other. They will have the same ethics, business beliefs and experiences as you and will be there to act as a sounding board at any point in your business life.

I have a small group of like minded colleagues and business owners on speed dial. When a problem comes up, I can choose the best one to pour out my concerns or ideas to. There is no competition between us and I know they will call me when *they* have an issue that they need an opinion on.

Sometimes we might call each other for a chat to confirm how trade is or plans for the next quarter. We gain a greater understanding by sharing our experiences. Many chief executives, finance directors and chairman of large corporate organisations also share ideas and frustrations in the same way — so far as the rules allow. They understand the virtue of this informal dialogue. The world would not spin without these communications.

The virtue of administration backup

The good ship Keith would not sail smoothly without support. There should be a saying: *Behind every good person is a great administrator.*

Some industry administration systems and the people that use them are fantastic. They maintain a tolerance, which can cater for your mistakes and correct them when they appear. I appreciate that you won't be in shock at this stage as I have detailed many of my own wrong turns. We *all* make mistakes and it takes a good administrator to work with you to correct these.

After all, without the marketing, sales, administration, completions and banking, the sales machine fails. But the simpler the sales administration process is for you, the client and the administrator, the lower the costs for the company and the greater the success and profit. That is what business is all about.

The opposite can be true of a *poor* system or administrator. If you're going to be a salesperson for any company, take a detailed look at their forms, sales brochures and information, processes and the quality of their service to ensure that it meets your own expectations and values. After all, you are the one that is going to be helping filling in the forms with the clients; *you* will have to be confident with them. Before you sign the employment contract, are you confident that you could get your client to sign the application form?

Industry qualifications

Most of my industry exams were achieved between 1994 and 2007 and are pertinent to this period and my future experiences.

Let me state for the record that industry qualifications are of limited use without industry *experience*. They teach you the rules and regulations, the tax angles and complications of products and the options available for advice, and this is important. What exams don't teach you is the application of these technical points to a client and their circumstances. This, in my opinion, only comes with experience.

As we approach a new era in the demands of providing financial advice, the issue of the level and relevance of qualifications comes to the fore and will only increase in the near future. Should it be experience that counts, or qualifications more than experience, or both?

The combination of the two is very powerful. This argument may not rage for much longer because the minimum levels of qualifications are being set and 'grandfathering' (where time and experience in the industry are deemed to have the same value as qualifications) does not seem to the regulatory authorities to be prudent or viable. The industry overall seems to be an older person's profession, and few people are keen on studying at a late stage in life.

Some people take the attitude that 'if it's not broken then don't fix it'. In addition, for some exams, the situation is not helped by institutions introducing high (and mandatory) charges to sit exams. This can have the effect of pushing eminently suitable and enthusiastic people away from our industry for the sake of profit.

Having undertaken many of the exams known to our industry, my advice would be: *don't just use one exam board or institution for your studies.*

I failed a few exams on the first attempt; not because of limited learning capacity but because I did not answer in the style required. After some time, I began to realise that each examination board has its own distinct style to achieve qualifications, some better and broader than others, and you may find that one suits you more than another. For any examination board, you should learn the content separately from learning their preferred style. This can be achieved by purchasing past exam papers. Further information on the options available to you can be found in the Resources section at the end of this book.

Experiment with different exam boards. There is no single answer to the financial services industry exams, so look around. Making it easy on yourself is half the battle.

Of course exams are important — but it is their application to the real world that is the real test of a true financial planner. It takes skill but this is true of any professional in business. Having a qualification and then using it are two different things. This is the old argument about whether you learn in order to pass exams or to improve yourself and your understanding. There is no point in passing an exam to display a certificate and do little else.

I once met a lady who had just qualified in her chosen field at the age of 22, although she had already been working in the industry for five years. She was delighted to qualify, and admitted that she had reached the pinnacle of her achievements and needed to do nothing more to make her a happy camper for the rest of her life. Personally, I'd always thought of receiving a qualification as the beginning of a career, rather than the end of any aspiration.

If you are taking a qualification, think about where it will take you — or where it, in combination with your own thirst for success, will take you. Then strive to exceed this personal goal.

Always remember though, Too much work and not enough play can make you dull...especially in the insurance world.

Many university graduates see the end of their degree course as the start of their career, rather than just the end of exams. They are looking to join a dynamic environment offering excellent prospects.

Having taken on a graduate a while ago, I was able to share my own financial services experience while testing his resolve to achieve qualifications. After four months of employment, my graduate had completed the base exams and moved on to the next level.

There is always the risk that graduates will be whisked away by the 'big guns' because, once qualified, they can be a valuable commodity, generating quality income. This is something that must be accepted. But if a graduate is thus launched into the industry as a professional financial planner, rather than a pushy product-focused salesperson, that is a small price.

I hope that the proposals from the Financial Services Authority for the new clearly defined distribution methods for retail UK financial advice (for both the public and employees) will attract more graduates to make the profession an even more vibrant place. This would be good for us as professionals and for our clients, too.

The relevance of learning can appear later

I was no academic at school and the tests of time, such as marriage, mortgages and divorce do little to aid leaning.

As a mature student of 37, I undertook a degree course in Financial Services at Napier University. In one trimester, we studied the profile and management style of Sir Fred Goodwin, the former chief executive of the Royal Bank of Scotland. He certainly was a focused and driven man. Various texts indicated that his management style was: 'go to your task and not deviate until finished'. Based on the successful clients and people that I have met, whatever profession or industry they follow, this strategy works.

To take a degree as a mature student is an interesting task because of the additional workload you agree to undertake whilst juggling the normal demands of your work and home life, if there is one.

Sobering thoughts

While I was writing this book, my father-in-law died.

He was 85 and a very humble and caring man. He had had a great life, serving in the Royal Marines in the Second World War. He became a lay reader, becoming part of the fabric of the community that he served in. He had the conviction of his values and held to these, and I respected him for this.

Bereavement is a sobering experience for any family — but it brings with it the burden of understanding that alongside death comes ongoing life, and that the younger generation must take the next step up on the conveyor belt of seniority in this life. It also requires a family member to understand the finances of the person who has died, whilst caring for the needs of the widow or widower and the rest of the family.

It also focuses the mind on financial planning and the real value you extract from investments during your lifetime.

Years ago, I was under the impression that the retirement age of 65 was invented by Chancellor Bismarck of

Germany. My understanding of the 'inventor' was correct but the suggested age was originally 70. Germany became the first nation in the world to use an old-age social insurance programme, which it adopted in 1889. This was indeed created by Chancellor Otto von Bismarck. The retirement idea was first proposed on the grounds that *'those who are disabled from work by age and invalidity have a well-grounded claim to care from the state'*.

Germany initially set age 70 as the retirement age and it was not until 27 years later in 1916 that it was lowered to 65. By that time, Bismarck had been dead for 18 years. It is interesting that, with greater longevity now in the UK population, the state pension age has started to rise from age 65.

My father-in-law was 85 when he died. As any actuary will tell you, this is approximately one year over the average for a middle class man with pension benefits. Actuaries can be excitable chaps.

This suggests a few observations:

- The day you take your pension benefits does not affect the day you will die. My father-in-law had 25 years of retirement. He was a fortunate man. He had benefited from the annuity pool he joined at the age of 60. Many people die early in their retirement, subsidising this pool. So, think carefully before deferring your pension — it might be too late. I would normally want to see a client have a 20-year window, to extract the value from a pension.

- These wise words come to you from me at the tender age of 43. I may sound like a schoolboy saying this, but the chances are, my half time whistle has already blown, and I am in the changing rooms being bawled out by the manager about the fact that my personal performance has not been good enough in the first half of life and that if I don't buck up my game I will lose the match. If *you* are going to have 20 years at retirement, then you only have 20 years or so more years of working life to put away enough money to be able to enjoy your twilight.

- And what about your clients? Where are they in *their* life cycle? Are they climbing, aspiring, satisfied or resigned? Understand this part of their life stage quickly. You won't find the question listed on your pro-forma questionnaire. You need to see and experience your clients for yourself, to understand where they are and empathise.

Santa Claus is coming to town

I was the youngest in a family. My mother coped well with the children running around the house, although she kept us in tow where she could.

When it came to birthdays, especially when we were young, we were frequently reminded that as the matriarch of the family, *her* present was to be something special and personal. As we got older, and after some years' practice, this became a straightforward task, but not without its time demands to ensure that you got it right.

This later experience was honed from the mistakes of my earlier life. Buying a cooking pan or gardening gloves was not a good idea; these were deemed to be household items and too impersonal for the birthday project. Havoc could be created if you got it wrong.

One late November I received an enquiry from a gentleman in an expensive part of Berkshire, asking to know the speed with which a new contribution could be made to a pension policy for his wife. This was very specific and became an *order take* rather than a sale: was there enough time to have the policy documents for 24th December? The reason he asked was because the policy documents were a Christmas present! I was somewhat bewildered by this manifestation of generosity towards a loved one but was in no position to query this underwhelming expression of love.

What possesses a man to think that such a trinket, a pension policy document, would be top of her Christmas wish list?

I suggest you *don't* try this at home; as your spouse's eyes may light up on Christmas morning with something that is *not* delight as her fingers caress the post 88 personal pension policy numbers you have so carefully selected. However shiny the plastic wallet that the policy documents come in, it's maybe not the choice of a loved one who was expecting something more personal on the 25th December, however useful for their dotage. They may have anticipated more focussed attention from you as they rip at the wrapping paper next to the Christmas tree and have to reach for a large glass of sherry when they realise what they have received.

Remember, a personal pension is for life, not just for Christmas.

Chapter 12 in a nutshell

Being involved in office banter and camaraderie is well worthwhile, and its value should not be underestimated. True business life friends are very valuable. Always remember that and treasure their wisdom.

Does the administration sales process meet with your values and expectations? You need to be confident that the sale you are making to your client is going to complete.

Spread you studies and exams around institutions and awards. This provides a greater perspective of our industry and, in my opinion, gives a student greater understanding. This will help with the quality of client advice you give and the sales you achieve.

Sign here, here and here!...

13. The Job Hoppers' Ball

As testament to how *not* to do your career a favour, I had a quick succession of employers — three in three years. A second marriage came and went in this period and it raises the question of where and what I was trying to achieve during this time in most aspects of my life. Was this a mid life crisis or another search for a better format to run my life? A lot of soul searching went on in this period and, as you will see, a few wrong turns were taken.

This in itself is worth learning from: understanding the employment proposition being chased is just as important as getting the job, even if the role you take on changes once you get there.

Change, along with divorce, became a significant period of learning for me, and that can never be a bad thing.

Independent financial advice

This was not my first foray into independent advice, of course. I had been a trainee mortgage broker with an independent agent who sold out the business to an insurance company within six months of my joining, way back in the 1980's.

This new role, however, was a different kettle of fish and did not involve mortgages. Having been made redundant, I had received a settlement and felt relaxed about my new situation. In hindsight, relaxing in your thirty-something years is not a good thing. I was about to remarry for the second time and the world seemed to be a brighter place, although the cost of the wedding (and the previous divorce) were still attacking the once plump bank account.

I bought a large black Jaguar XJ saloon with a personalised plate on it and wafted around the lanes of Surrey trying not to scratch the silky paintwork. I thought it was great, with the interior bathed in leather and wood, but one or two clients thought it was a bit over the top to say the least. I am sure you could pull away from the traffic lights and see the fuel gauge move down.

Now what does Jeremy Clarkson say about cads, bounders and Jags?

My position now was in financial services sales and marketing. My first objective was to achieve sales for the company (and quickly to cover my costs) and then to consider the marketing and improving overall communication of the business. Both responsibilities were attractive and I was bursting with enthusiasm — and there were possible equity prospects for the future if things worked out.

The management team was very fair and keen to do the right thing; that should always be applauded. There was little talking and lots of focused *doing*, just the way it should be. However, moving from a big corporate to a small independent is a change in cultures and one that needed some adjustments on both sides.

My main issue with my employment — and it was *my* issue rather than theirs — was that I felt I was trying to replicate the environment of a big corporate, and the organisation was simply never going to fit this model. The independence of the advice was worthwhile and added to the poignancy of offering a balanced approach to clients, rather than the tied-agent model I had followed for the previous twelve years.

This might have been a good place for me to stay but frustration with the progression process overcame me. I wanted to move the business on more quickly than could be realistically achieved. My irritation began to grow, and with it my desire to leave.

It was time for the Jag to go as I moved to London and an Audi arrived. Far more practical and ironically also better for moving me out when the second divorce proceedings began.

Another wrong turn: a tied representative again

This proved to be a ten-month disappointment for all parties.

Other than keeping me working in London and 'The Square Mile' — which in my line of work has to be done at least once in your working lifetime — this change proved to be a disappointment. I had anticipated a similar life to that of the last large corporate I had worked for, but this was not to be the case. I became a representative of a single company offering good quality products by various distribution methods, including a direct sales division.

Working in London, just as the second Gulf War was starting (March 2003) raised concerns about public safety. The media were full of the rhetoric of George W Bush and 'weapons of mass destruction'. I'm sure the world is a safer place now we have President Obama.

I had visited London for weekly client meetings for many years. However, to work there full time was an experience — there are those who might call it drudgery, plugged into my radio listening to Chris Tarrant and tapping my feet to Beyonce, who was apparently *Crazy in Love*— and I can tick the box to say I did that for two years. It does provide a greater level and diversification of experience, and you should take the chance go and do it for as long as you can endure.

This new employer maintained a significant management structure and a robust sales process at every stage of the client presentation. For me, this came back to the old issue: *would you ask your relative to sign up to the concepts and processes being offered — and if not, why not?*

A previous employer had taught me a valuable lesson about the importance of taking the client with you during the co-ordinated sales process to make sure that they understand what is going on and where they stand in the overall process. Good signposting if you like. If you lose the client along the way you may lose the overall sale and, perhaps, the client as well.

The new training programme, in my opinion, was elaborate and company process-driven which took a long time to complete. In fairness to the company, after more than 18 years in the industry by that time it was always going to be tough for them to 'train' me — and I believe my skills and experience are why they had hired me in the first place.

It must be admitted at this point that my job-hopping was not saying good things about my character and commitment to any employer. It was also personally wearing. It was time for me to get the next move right. But where should I go next and what distribution model would I favour? This is a personal choice and one that only you can make and be comfortable with. But seeking out the best for you may take a lifetime or you may get it right first time. But getting right for you is what it's all about. Personally, I know I am there now.

Independent financial advice… again!

For my next job hop I went back to offering independent advice, this time remaining in London. The employment offer made was attractive, from an independent with strong presence in the advice market I favoured, retirement planning. But it proved to be my final lesson that I only had one long-term option available to me . . .

The new position was with a professional firm in London. It was a high quality organisation, with people who were shrewd at dealing with good business, both in terms of quantity and quality. Personally, I had lost a little confidence by now because of the personal pressures of divorce and 'job hopping' and needed to settle into my sales stride for the future; for *my* future.

I was optimistic and my enthusiastic arrival went well. I had built a small client following of my own and the company had a client bank that needed to be 'farmed', so I quickly got on the phone and started filling the diary. I had learned the power of the client telephone contact in my formative years of mortgage broking and now it worked well for me.

Production started quickly and smoothly, all according to plan — however, my personal lingering doubt about my own long-term future remained. I worked towards the needs of the employer as required but I was starting to focus on what I really wanted to achieve.

Reading this, some of you may be saying: 'You idiot! Start your own business, you should have done it years ago!' I was not ready to do that yet. However, within three months of starting this new role, I knew it was time. This was a personal discovery, something that could not be taught. The people I was working with were good people, and some of the very best — but I wanted more from my career.

My final employment 'hop' washed away the scales of blindness to what could be achieved with a bit of application on my part. New thinking started to occupy my mind, usually on the morning and evening train to and from London.

The leaving party was great fun and many ales were consumed.

I had a new partner, Esther, now my (third) wife and she had also gone through a divorce. A green Mondeo was the practical choice of the time, great car. We had both rather been through the mill and together we focussed on what we as a couple wanted to achieve from the depths that we had plunged too after our mutual separations. This time did feel a little bit like we had our backs against the wall with no way out and some significant and positive action needed to be taken to recover any comfortable future lifetime.

Chapter 13 in a nutshell

The benefit of a small company is that it can be quick in both decision-making and action. Medium or large corporate organisations cannot usually achieve this. That's why, especially in the UK, smaller companies are so successful.

Understand the remuneration package and the process of its training application to understand the potential of 'on target earnings'. And when you think you have got it straight, read it again carefully.

Don't be a prisoner in any position you hold.

Sign here, here and here!...

14. You didn't mean to do that, did you?

The 'realistic' black sheep

When you are setting your sales target or negotiating your sales for the next quarter, or year, do you find that being *realistic* is seen as negativity by the powers that be?

It doesn't help that many of your colleagues have crumbled under pressure from their own meetings with their manager and nodded gamely at every unachievable target set before them. Therefore, when you throw in some realism about what is *achievable*, a few raised eyebrows come to the fore. This is when you start to be seen as the 'black sheep' of the sales team. Taking it a stage further, by taking a stand you may be thought not to be a team player. And if the team doesn't meet its target, it will be your *sole* responsibility.

The reality is that your sales manager has been sitting in his or her sales director's office, responding like a nodding dog to suggestions of what is achievable — even though the sales director may have limited perception of what is going on in the locality.

You can see them now; they look a bit like the insurance hound nodding away, but at the wheel of their superior model BMW rather than on the parcel shelf.

There is a careful line to tread here. You need to be realistic about what is achievable, *and* cohesive enough to veil your realism in a way that ensures the sales manager understands your thought process and buys into your thinking and suggestions.

This works for both you and the manager. When your process is going well, you should be the first to push your targets up. When times are hard, you must still negotiate to achieve your objectives but have a realistic handle on the likely outcome for your target.

Whatever you do, make sure you *add value*, both personally and for the business.

Which distribution model?

To further your career, you need to ask yourself three things:

- *Where next?*

- *With whom?*

- *Is the business outlet you choose going to be tied or an independent offering?*

When deciding to move on, you have the conviction that it is time for change, usually while you are still with your old employer. It's up to you to put that right. Look at your current sales offering: would you buy it? If the answer is *no*, then new horizons beckon. Never lie to yourself.

I also asked myself:

- *Is it me?*

- *Am I the problem with this job?*

- *If I changed my attitude, would things improve, or is it never going to fit my prescribed model?*

- *Am I bothered?*

Some people call me Tigger, always bouncing off the walls, always up for a challenge, with a 'have a go, go, go' attitude. Don't underestimate how important your attitude can be. I believe I got this drive from my childhood, having been born with Spina Bifida — but we each get our drive from something. After many corrective operations in Oxford, I always felt that I could do better, and was out to prove that I could. The Spina Bifida was in a mild form, although I will always walk with a limp, and the running can also look rather strange too.

This desire to perform drives my wife up the wall. 'Why can't you just relax, just do nothing?' she wails. If I move my head correctly, generally in a nodding movement, my selective deafness seems to cut in at that point! Or is that just a man thing?

I don't want to be average. I don't want to head back to the 1970s, where the populace had 2.4 children and a Ford Cortina. That was not what I and many other aspiring individuals were about. I at least aspired to a Ford Granada with a vinyl roof! It sounds a bit like the Sweeney, with the Bay City Rollers belting out of the new style cassette deck in the dashboard.

Where is your station in life? Are you Mondeo Man or do you aspire higher? I love Ford Mondeos — but I don't drive one anymore.

You may remember the *gut feel* that I referred to earlier. Go with that, because invariably it's the right instinct. When you decide to move employments, which distribution model and corresponding company do you choose next? Do you become another sales representative, working as a tied agent, or do you go back to being independent? Have you tried both already?

Imagine it was your relative sitting in front of you: which option would they prefer? If you don't know, go and ask them; do your own survey. Will this decision be the same when the FSA has shaken up the industry to clarify the channels of UK distribution for the consumer?

Consider the following:

• Does the income and the way this is provided (salary/commission/bonus/combination) that you receive from each channel matter to you?

• Does this affect your shorter or longer-term decisions?

• And what about the financial needs of your family? Will this dictate how you negotiate his package?

• Is a company car needed?

• Do you need childcare vouchers?

• What do you need?

Moving around employers as much as I did is not a good long-term strategy. You need to find a home, a true home; the sooner you find it, the better. Think carefully about how the distribution model you choose is likely to change in the future.

Future distribution models— are they right for you?

With financial education now being introduced in secondary schools, it is to be hoped that the general public will become money-savvy about their basic needs. The proliferation of the Internet will help that understanding, and expand it to allow a significant percentage of the public to undertake their own basic financial planning without the need for direct advice from providers or advisers.

We have already seen guides to making long-term investment decisions, such as *decision trees*. These allow individuals to follow a flow chart to see what product meets their needs, if at all.

Some people suggest that the banks will also grow their advice sector and thus their market segment in the process. I also believe that, in the same way that many supermarkets and retail consumer organisations offer deposit accounts in competition with banks, the banks will also see competition from independent financial advice websites and insurance companies for financial advice offerings.

At the time of finishing this book, the current government was actively pursuing the devolution of the current bank network to other organisations. A good example is the recent application from the organisation *Virgin* for a bank licence, and also purchasing a bank to use as a vehicle for their plans.

You might decide at this point that the writing is on the wall and it's time to abandon the profession. However, it is my belief that the financial advice market is going to become more competitive over time, and that it will offer even greater rewards to the right individuals and companies.

Look at the financial strength of any organisation that you join, to ensure that it is still going to be around when and if these new regulatory demands come about. Ask to see the company accounts; it's every bit as reasonable a request as asking a client how much they earn or how much they have borrowed.

What do you want to achieve with a new role?

- *Management?*
- *Sales success without the responsibility of management?*
- *Or is it just a job?*

Take time to decide before you start your career move process and set yourself your own business plan.

I ordered it on the web

Running our own business, my wife and I have learned about competing on the Internet with the big boys. We have been running two services for the past three years, www.advicemadesimple.com and www.planmypension. co.uk. Never let anyone tell you that the Internet simply can't compete with face-to-face advice; it can, but in a different way.

Is the UK ready for online financial advice?

The first attempt at creating an online financial advice market was in late 1990 and no longer exists. In addition, using the car/household/insurance website examples, it is interesting to view the statistic available. Comparison websites are referred to as *aggregators* in the trade, and reduce customer time spent trawling the wider Internet for information:

- Around 65 per cent market share car insurance/ Confused.com (2007)

- £36.7 million profit, a rise of around 59% in 2007/ Admiral for its website, Confused.com

- Estimated 15 million users of comparison sites per month (2008)

- Moneysupermarket.com valued at around £1 billion (2007)

To maintain market share, profit and distribution penetration, many companies have diversified into other markets, such as financial services *product sales* rather than mere *advice*.

Another sector that has pounced upon this penetration opportunity, away from their core business, is the major supermarkets that have large distribution power, with many having introduced financial services as a new offering.

We are all growing older, and the Internet is the tool of choice for many clients. It's the same for the youngsters as it is for the *Silver Surfers*, who have embraced this technology over the last decade or so. The current *Baby Boomers* seem to know no bounds when it comes to the Internet. Ease of use will increasingly become more important to customers than the personal relationships that your business was originally based on. In a way this is sad. However, I can see that this is progress and a way of developing the overall offerings available.

Your personal three-year business plan

In any new role, you would normally set yourself a three-year strategy.

You will spend the first year finding your feet and selling as much as you can to cover your costs, probably making a few errors along the way.

In the second year you should start to blossom, with significant sales success — and a growing depth of understanding of your organisation, its foibles, cultures and the objectives of the management structure within which you work.

The third year is where you should see the cash rolling in. It sounds mercenary — but you're a salesperson and that's what you are there to achieve. It is likely that you will see your sales plateau in or at the end of this year and this is likely to set the trend for the future.

The following sales projection assumes a reasonable average anticipated sales production process for a good representative, resulting in £175,000 per annum production:

- Year 1: £ 90,000   -   Finding your feet

- Year 2: £135,000   -   Growing understanding

- Year 3: £180,000   -   Plateau

- Year 4: £185,000   -   (Adding in a bit for inflation)

Don't let me stop you doing what you're doing, if you think that this example doesn't represent your style; the 'average' detailed above could be for another member of your team. There has to be a shining light in any sales team — if that is you, I admire your prowess. However, if you are the team average or *also-ran*, who might struggle to achieve these production levels, then I believe that reading this book will focus your mind on which areas you need to develop.

A good manager should anticipate a production curve for a new member of the sales team as suggested above — but make sure that this is agreed at the outset of your appointment in order to manage your expectations, along with theirs. There is nothing more frustrating than working for a new organisation and doing well, while naturally comparing yourself with the well-established salesperson producing three times as much as you without breaking sweat.

The three-year plan helps put all this in context, especially when you start to beat your high flying colleagues in the second year. That turnaround keeps these *others* on their toes. Don't hang onto your BMW keys for too long!

Perhaps you had ideas of further roles in management or promotion, (despite the risks I warned you about!)? In this case, you may want to start your move towards this goal at the end of the third year or thereabouts. When you accept a promotion, the three-year clock starts again.

I have seen many medium-sized and larger companies using this strategy because they believe it gives their team the optimal time to perform, whilst also keeping them fresh and, to some extent, on their toes. I understand that other organisations such as the military use a similar process for their officers, with tours of duty lasting around the same time; after that, a change may be made to allow a new perspective to be undertaken.

Time to think

When was the last time you took time to think about what you are trying to achieve? Either personally or professionally? This is an opportunity to remind yourself of your overall strategy and why you are doing what you are doing.

Assuming you do take the time, *when* do you do this? Some would describe this as a *strategy meeting or a brain dump*. Whatever you choose to call it, this is a process of clearing your mind-path of the clutter and trivia that you gather over time, to focus on new objectives or refocus on older goals and aspirations.

Whatever you do, wherever you find yourself both physically and in your overall life journey, take time to think. It is never too late.

It is vital that you do take time to revisit your objectives to ensure that they are not lost in the mist of sales targets, meetings and everything else.

How often do you do this thinking? Once a week? Once a month? Every quarter? It's up to you, so long as don't miss out on what you want to do. You only have one life and the clock is ticking. You cannot reclaim the time you have spent. Whatever you do, make sure you will have no regrets.

Life is something to be embraced, not just something that happens to you. Wring every last drop out of each day!

When you have secured this time to think about you … what exactly are you going to think about?

Will you be *forensic*, looking at the minutiae of today's problem? Or will you take a *thematic* approach to this quarter's successes and failings? Or will you take a more *global* view of 'planet you', considering bigger issues about your future and how you want your life to unfold? Or all of the above?

Ideally, you should take a little of each approach into every thinking session you have. In my opinion the global approach is the most important, as it may change your entire perspective on your future — and that could start today.

Are you going to stay with your employer/house/spouse or are you going to start afresh: start your own company/ move house/get divorced? As a personal recommendation, don't try all of these issues at once folks, it could get awfully messy!

This introduces what I call *life junctions*. I will consider these with you further in the following pages.

Frustration: your best lesson

As you have seen from the changes I've made in my own career, at one point I was becoming unemployable. Does this ring alarm bells for you?

With hindsight, I can now see that it was I who was maturing rather than any employer being obstructive. I *should* have realised that this meant it was time to start a business of my own.

This step is not appropriate for everyone. Many people never reach this point and stay employed. We are all different, with different personal requirements and objectives. Starting out on your own is a big decision — but well worth it in my case.

It was disappointing that so much of my motivation to start a business came from *frustration*. I felt disillusioned by companies, and their struggle to offer a consistent high-quality service to clients, year after year.

The desire for each company to be better, brighter and bigger usually saw average-quality initiatives going off half-cocked, only to be cancelled six months later. This would happen after several clients had been through the new process or sales push, only to be left high and dry.

When you treat staff, clients and prospects that way, you end up with departing personnel and single-purchase customers who have not enjoyed the sales process and never buy again. This is not a sustainable business model.

Your hardest lessons are usually the best to learn from, however bitter the pill. I learned more from an average manager than a good one, and I am pleased to confirm that there are a few brilliant managers out there. Both have their part to play in allowing you to focus on what you want to achieve. A good manager will play to your strengths and guide you to improve on areas that can be developed.

He may demonstrate by his actions or by pointing you to training guides and qualifications. However the good ones do it, they want the best from you and for you. An average manager may not give you that level of encouragement, however this in itself should provide you with a challenge to succeed. Frustration can be as effective a tutorial as any classroom training session. As you can tell, I have benefitted from both management styles.

Although frustration is a difficult emotion to embrace, remember to take the positives from it. *What could be done better? Why does something not work?* This converts your irritation into a challenge to solve the problem.

There are times when a situation or a person is an obstacle you are not going to get around. How long will it stand in the way of your progress towards what you truly believe is yours? Take the initiative to solve it, even if that means leaving and starting afresh elsewhere, either on your own or with a new employer. As an example, it reminds me of cabinet ministers resigning from a sinking ship because of a Prime Minister who simply does not understand when it is time to let go.

A visit I once made to a client's house provides an example of an unusual frustration. Frances was a focussed but approachable lady. The demands of the family were significant, but they had sufficient funds to cover most of their desires. The house was set in three acres and they had an indoor swimming pool in a separate building. I laughed when I saw the sign on the door, which matched the family's sense of humour and read as follows: *"Welcome to my ool. Please note that there is no 'P' in the word 'ool'. Please keep it that way!"* Humour washer way of trying to control the issue that frustrated her.

Try dealing with your frustrations. Simply taking a different stance on a situation will change your attitude to the issue and that could be half the battle. And if your personal attitude to a situation is half the battle, it could be argued that half the situation lies with you, rather than with the issue at hand.

I have watched someone treat a serious situation with such arrogance that the situation simply disappeared — because it was believed that he didn't care anyway. It worked for him because he didn't get tied down by a situation or an individual.

Whether this is right or not is a different question. For him, it was a solution.

Chapter 14 in a nutshell

Understand the three-year business or sales structure and work with it to your best advantage. You will feel it happening to you as you progress. You will know whether you are ready for the next three-year structure. Your promotion beckons – but don't forget that it is only a stepping stone to the next promotion.

Life will happen to you if you let it. Don't. Ensure that you steer it in the direction you want to go with gusto each day!

Learn at every opportunity and event in your life. You choose the subject and lesson, but keep on learning. Some say you can't teach an old dog new tricks. You can if you give a 'Pooch' a biscuit! Try it.

The hardest lessons that you learn are usually the best to learn from, however bitter the pill you have to swallow.

Sign here, here and here!...

15. Time for a new horizon

One strange day

One day, you must have reached a point in your life when the thought went through your mind: *No! I am not doing this anymore.*

There may have been a quick process leading to this momentous day, or it may have crept up on you. The subject might be your employment, your company, your marriage, a house — anything that affects your life. Whatever the issue, you will remember *that day.*

For me, it's happened a few times on varying subjects, namely divorce and employment. My second book is my personal and professional view on divorce, and its painful challenges from a financial perspective. This chapter concentrates on *that day* in employment terms.

That day was when I decided to start my own business.

To set the scene, I had come out of a second divorce and was settled with my partner, Esther. I had enjoyed a good lifestyle, supported by good income and realised that if that was going to continue I was less likely to achieve it as an employee.

I am not sure that it was an *exciting* day; this enormous decision was born out of sheer frustration. However, it was a process of deduction to reach the decision that the only way forward for me was to start my own company.

When you reach *that day*, it may be as straightforward for you too.

My own business

This has proved to be the best bit of my career so far. I don't believe it's the finale — but you already know that!

I am sure you will have worked out by now that I have an ego and that I believe I can do a better job than anyone else. While I realise that this belief is probably not the case, it is not a bad opinion to maintain as a starting point when you want to go it alone.

You find out very quickly how alone you are, when the doors open for new business on the first day.

Thinking you are good at what you do, starting a business on the back of that thought, and then making it pay, are three very different situations. These thoughts need to be considered very carefully before taking the leap of faith.

As you know, I had become frustrated with previous employers and particularly with their management processes, ethics and styles. I believed I could do better.

You may have a wealth of experience that clients can rely on and trust. You may have many industry qualifications and skills to get the job done. So what? That is why you have been employed in the past. Employers hired you to achieve quality sales to allow them to get on with their work, which was running the business that employed you. Having now run a business of my own for a while, I can now appreciate the magnitude of their task. However, at the time I certainly could not see the issues they faced. Part of their extensive role is to identify the correct talent and to bring it to their company — not to do the selling and advice work that you are so good at.

Gradually it became clear that my previous frustrations were growing pains rather than an issue of being good at my work. Everyone knew I could offer a high quality and compliant sales offering; it now became a matter of who was going to keep the profits of this labour.

It was only the generosity and maturity of my last employer, in providing me with the respect and freedom to let me effectively run my own business within his, that allowed me to see past the frustration to what I could achieve. For this I am profoundly grateful.

I have heard many people say that they wish that they had started their own business years before they actually did. I have never said this because I realise I was not ready until that point. At 37, when I started the company, I was young enough to have sufficient stamina to see the process through — but, at the same time, experienced enough to know how to make the new business project pay.

The *junction* in anyone's life, where they start you're their own company, is an important one. Many people reach this *decision junction* but take another turning and stay employed. However, you don't want to condemn yourself in later life to regrets about what might have been.

This is a personal choice and one that needs to be thought through, right down in your soul. It's important because the personal commitment needed to run a company knows no end.

Are you ready? No regrets now.

Life junctions and noise

Life junctions, important situations that require a decision and a clear course of action, happen to us all, in every walk of life.

They start early. Do you go to university or the University of Life? Do you get married? Do you then get divorced? Do you procreate? Do you relocate or find a new job? Redundancy, bereavement, births; all can be life-changing situations.

I often go through this with clients as we consider together which direction they should take. We look at the routes available and then challenge the thinking to ensure that the planned journey is robust.

At this point, I must add an important note about the *objections* that will be made to the life decisions that you have agreed. This is because they will challenge the values of people around you. I call these 'interruptions' and the questioning of your personal thinking as 'noise'. Interruptions are a personal thing and can be whatever distracts you from your true thinking. From the kids nagging at you to parents providing you with the benefit of their wisdom to a manager pointing you in a direction you simply do not want to go. You will know where they come from and the noise they create.

Noise is something that confuses thinking and interrupts progress along the path you have chosen. You've usually made an informed and considered decision that suits you, your family and your overall circumstances the best —

and this should not be interfered with. Your decisions are based on your values and *noise* is usually someone else's belief that you should take on their values. Repel the boarders and avoid their 'noise'. After all, it is your life and the one person who lives it is you.

Following a divorce, I knew I had to make some serious changes to my own life and career if I was ever going to recover a pleasant standard of living and this was a *life junction* for me.

Esther was getting tired of me moaning about my unsatisfactory employment position and job-hopping and how I felt trapped. She too had gone through a divorce and had some funds available — and, most importantly, a belief in my abilities to perform as a businessman. You may remember the 'put up or shut up' speech by John Major, Conservative Prime Minister in the 1990s. His job was being threatened from within his own party and he took the calculated risk of challenging any detractors either to stand openly against him or to stand aside. My wife posed the same challenge to me. The options were to be a happy employee, have some money for other projects and 'shut up moaning!' . . .or 'have some of the money I'm offering you, start your own company and 'shut up moaning!'

'Whatever you do, just shut up moaning!' she said firmly, which is her prerogative.

Talking about and actually taking the jump of forming a new company are two very different things. The 'talking about starting a company' had come to an end and the doing part had to start. The new business started after ten solid months of planning. Business planning can take a long time and has to be tailored to the anticipated needs of the fledgling company. . In your planning, talk to everyone you trust and take their advice. You may not like their guidance but build it into your model anyway.

Esther had belief both in our joint abilities and the concept of the new business, filling a gap in the South East market, mainly around Surrey. She helped and bought in (literally) to the process and joined the company after three months, leaving her engineering role at London Underground.

We divided roles (marketing, sales, administration, web design, accounting, etcetera) and earmarked them specifically to ensure that each person had their own tasks and roles to focus on. This ensured that there was no duplication of effort, maximising productivity. Esther's eye for processes ensured that there was an easy transition to financial services. This agreement and understanding remains in place to this day.

For your business planning, you are likely to evaluate the situation and the components of the structure to start your own business. You consider the likelihood of success, just as if you were working towards a big sale: where, when, how, what. I think of these components as *pointers*, either positive or negative. Once evaluated, you can see which way the pointers are leading and the proportion of positives and negatives.

For me, they were all positive — but that is still not enough to take the leap of faith. You've got to have the courage of your convictions as well . . . and then 'Next year Rodney, we'll be millionaires!' Well maybe not. When you reach a *life junction* like this, look at your own *pointers*, both negative and positive. If you don't have the desire for it, then that is fine and honourable, but don't put yourself in a position where you can look back later and wonder what might have been. For many of us this *life junction* only appears once in your life, if at all.

The business plan had been drawn up and implemented as far as possible. Premises, marketing, branding, logo, press releases, letterheads, cash flow were all prepared and secured in readiness for the start date. We had also gained a licence to trade from the FSA, which had gone through in just eight weeks.

Take your time over the preparation; it's worth it. Get your business plan right at the outset and then you will have less extra business planning to do once you are trading. Going off half-cocked is a terrible situation and one from which many of the medium and large corporates suffer. It's probably one of the reasons why you left their employment in the first place.

As a small company you have to be smarter, more agile and more flexible than your competitors.

Cleaner, bookkeeper, networker, administrator and candlestick maker

Our doors opened on our shiny new office at 9.00am on October 4th, 2004. There was no orderly queue outside the front door of our office and the phones did not light up at the start of the day. I think the only call on the first day was Esther to ask if I was OK.

The economic climate was good at the time and forecasted prospects looked reasonable. This was set against a backdrop of an American election that would culminate in seeing George W Bush win his second Presidential Election in November and the loss of another President, Ronald Reagan in the summer.

Take it from me: a start-up is a lonely place to be and any trusted support should be welcomed. However, don't forget that if you are starting a small company then you are going to be chief cook and bottle washer. Although you started your company to offer 'X', in my case financial planning, you will also need to understand marketing, accounts, office utilities, banking and tax among others.

Get used to this idea. Many providers and professionals that you buy services from will let you down or try to overcharge you. Be ready for this. Trust no one until they have proved they can perform to your expectations.

Also, if you are working with colleagues, ensure that each role, task and requirement is written down and allocated appropriately. This avoids wasted energy through duplicated work. Each party needs to own their tasks to ensure success. You, as the boss, need to remember that if a project has been allocated to someone else then it is *not your department*.

Take it from me, though — this is not being a *jobsworth* like my experience in the bank. In *these* circumstances, it works. It allows you to concentrate on the issues that you excel in, and you can expend your energies to maximum advantage. Once you are established and start to build your staff base, you can cascade tasks to others. To the more autocratic of us, this is referred to as *giving orders* — and it is dangerous at most times, but a firm hand needs to be available and used where necessary to ensure the delivery of your business objectives. You need performance, but you also need to support those around you. You will have no time to maintain passengers in your company, especially in the current economic climate.

So, expect to be offering advice and negotiating sales at 9.00 am, seeing your accountant at 11.00 am, phoning the tax office at 1.00 pm, doing sales again at 2.00 pm, photocopying application forms at 3.00 pm and hoovering the office at 6.30 pm.

Be prepared for half a dozen sales calls a day offering to sell you water coolers, franking machines, pens, sales leads and other luxuries. These are tiresome at best and wearing at worst.

A cold start

The first three months of any new business are going to be interesting.

You will have created a business plan, your own thoughts and model, for the next two or three years. What is a business plan? It can really be anything that you want it to be — but by detailing every aspect of your expectations then it can be challenged, back-tested and confirmed before you start. This will provide a plan you can follow, to manage your expectations and ensure that you don't go mad in the first few months.

It is daunting when you see the first quarter's figures, noting limited income and vast outgoings. Our first January (after three months trading) looked awful. And it was! But because this 'low' in terms of income and capital had been carefully predicted in the business plan, I knew that we were on target, even if the target at that point looked dreadful. Some element of comfort could be drawn from the predicted process, rather than feeling I was running a bottomless pit of costs that would only end in oblivion.

A business plan might include the following:

- Income to be achieved in the first 12 months? 24 months? 36 months?

- Of this income, a breakdown by quarter in the first year (the first quarter will be bad!)

- Type of sales

- Number of sales

- Your target market and what is going to attract buyers to your door (marketing)

- Average sale size

- Expected outgoings and their required payment dates (such as rent quarterly in advance)

- Peak performance months

- Form of the business (Limited Liability Partnership, Partnership, Limited Company)

- Your expected income and its format (drawings, salary, dividends)

There are others available on the Internet that also provide some good examples of what you need to think about. However, you know what you are trying to achieve and you will need to tailor your plan accordingly.

My business plan list above is not exhaustive and you will also need to undertake the ever-important cash flow forecast for up to 36 months. These combined features should allow you to test your theories on overall income and profitability, or Key Performance Indicators (KPIs) if you prefer.

Keep your focus locked firmly on the sole aim of your business and map out your predictions on a time line.

One easy lesson I learned was to take the business plan forecast, halve the predicted sales, double the predicted costs and then plot this model. This takes any egotistical over-enthusiasm out of the plan and was actually closer to reality than I had anticipated.

If this business plan model holds true, even if it looks ugly, then you are probably on to a winner.

When you want to borrow money or arrange an overdraft, the bank will want to see your business plan to ensure that you are not going to waste both your and their time and money. A good way to find out whether your business plan works is to see whether your bankers would lend you money, even though you don't need any. If they *would*, then you know you are on the right track.

Like any good business plan, you will (and the bank will if you are endeavouring to borrow) look at various aspects of the overall approach.

First of all, why you? What experience do you have? Past performance is not a guarantee of future performance so why will you be able to continue your abilities in this new venture?

What funds do you need? How are you going to raise and more importantly repay these funds? At what cost and on which terms? When are the funds needed and how often?

You must understand cash flow and build a safety margin into your business plan.

How are you going to protect both your business and the funds injected into it if business goes a little slower that you anticipated?

My first sale was achieved in the November and the first income was paid in December, just before Christmas. As a friend put it: 'There will be butter on your parsnips this season!' There was, thank goodness, but this was soured by the terrible news of the tsunami in Thailand that followed the next day.

Having built your plan, don't forget the three-year rule on how the business is likely to mature. As a reminder, the first year will be spent running around getting set up and out there, the second year will start to see the business firm up with production possibly doubling, and the third year should see the true performance as all the building blocks are by then in place. Your strands of business strategies should be complete for marketing, sales, production, administration and compliance.

I wish you the best of luck in your new endeavour. If it goes well, within 24 months you will become completely unemployable and this could be your greatest compliment. I recently called a colleague who started his company at around the same time I did. He commented that he now felt that he 'would last around a whole half hour' in an employed post before he would explode, tell them that they were all rubbish, and resign.

Running a company does make you harder. You have to be decisive — and this is required of you every single day. Stand by the decisions you make and have conviction in your actions. (You might want to let your spouse or partner know this before you start.) I recommend the journey, although if you are looking for a peaceful life then don't start. You will learn more than you ever would as an employee and it will open doors that could never be accessed in the past.

Keep your feet on the ground and don't lose sight of the fact that this new process is all about your clients.

Remember your good clients

When things start to go well and your model starts to plateau, don't forget your clients. It was your ambition to provide a better service that started this ball rolling in the first place.

In the undulation of my employment transitions, I lost contact with a client who had appreciated the advice I'd offered in the past. Remember the 'people buy people' analogy. On setting up my own company, Rebecca contacted me. Out of character, as Rebecca was usually rather softly spoken, she sternly said something of great significance:

'Keith, you left me. Don't ever do that again,' and then she carried on with the conversation normally. She is still a client and I have learned my lesson. This is an example of how important the work that you provide to your clients is, and the trust that they place in you.

Most clients trust and respect you for your work, care and professionalism and this will build over the years that you know them. Never forget that you are in this business together. Without them you have no business.

The main point of client care, whatever type of business you run, is *communication*. Clients like to hear from you, they want to know what's happening in your world, what's interesting, what might be relevant to them or what is specific to them. Make sure that you keep them posted regularly — even when things go wrong.

I will talk about marketing at length in the next chapter. If, like me, you enjoy marketing, then make sure that this task is allocated to you at the outset of your business because it does take energy.

Fire

You can never leave your baby, the company you created, even though your spouse expects you to leave it behind when you enter the plane bound for some sunny shore. With the introduction of Netbooks and 'on the move email', the office comes with you and is only neglected for as long as the flight lasts.

As an example, we went on holiday to an outlying island in the Bahamas. It rained most of the time, which rather dampened the overall mood. However, on landing, I reached for the phone-cum-computer to retrieve my emails and messages. We then discovered that the mobile phone provider we used did not cover the area we were visiting. Nightmare!

After a few hours of panic, I found that the only way of communicating with the office was to use the hotel computer (when a slot was available) to log into my email account. Because of the different time zones, the time delay was around eight hours.

We had left a young staff member, a school leaver from the summer, in charge of the office during the quiet Christmas period. A senior person emailing to ask what's happening while he's away can be tiresome, if not downright tedious, even for someone who has a mature head on her shoulders. Therefore the odd email question asking about the progress of the day's communications was not well received and received curt email responses.

'Good morning. What's happening in the office today?' I asked her.

'Everything's fine,' came the terse reply.

Eventually, I got angry at the lack of detail and emailed accordingly: 'I do not want to know that everything is *fine*. I want to know what's in the post? Who has visited the office? Who has telephoned? If the office has burnt down!' was my rather puerile message.

This email was sent at around 11pm, Bahamian time, and I went to bed. I was able to log in around nine o'clock the next morning, again using the hotel computer.

The email subject was headed, 'Fire'.

It read as follows: 'The building two doors down is on fire and this is spreading. Have been asked to evacuate and will keep you updated . . .'

The irony of the two emails together became rather unamusing. The email was sent at about 10am, UK time. The woman concerned was then locked out of the office for another eight hours. This left us in the dark for a day in the Bahamas. The following day, an explanatory email explained what had happened. In fact, it had been quite a big fire and scary for all concerned.

It showed both the power and the failings of the technology that we rely on.

Any incident, however small or large, focuses the mind of a business owner on the ability to trade in the event of a system failure — whether that be a personal situation (ill health) or an operational failure (fire or water damage, computer failure). You should always be mindful of these potential horrors, and plan to be able to provide continuity to your clients, your regulator and yourself.

Be prepared and don't forget to test your plan to ensure it works.

Chapter 15 in a nutshell

Thinking you are good, starting your own business on the back of that belief, and then making it pay are three very different situations. Understand and plan for this.

Think carefully when you reach the junction of changing your career. You will reach your junction; it's only a matter of time. Check and re-check the viability of this change before taking your jump.

Be ready to be a Jack-of-all-trades; to an extent you will also have to be a master of all.

Communication is the key. Clients want to hear from you so keep them posted regularly.

Sign here, here and here!...

16. Marketing, my favourite subject

Don't be afraid; marketing is not a swear word. It might prove to be a bit of an ego trip — but so is setting up or running your own business, and you don't have a problem with that, do you? I have detailed through the course of the book the theory that 'people buy people'. This can be reflected through your marketing and is a reflection of the personality that is your business.

The simplest thing is to sell yourself. If you cannot get people to buy *you*, then you are starting on a sticky wicket. What do I mean by 'sell yourself'? I mean having a personable manner that attracts and retains attention from the buying public. It's as if the public were asking: 'What's interesting about you and your offer?'

Try it. Put together a presentation to your family on the subject of you. Make it about you, your strengths and areas for development (what we used to call weaknesses!), your objectives and aspirations and what motivates you. This should not be a 'how great I am' show, but a professional presentation that shows empathy with your audience, that wins their interest and confidence in a time bound process, say five minutes. Ask them to judge it and suggest ways to improve it.

You will find this exercise useful (and amusing) and it will come in handy at a future time when, out of the blue, you are asked to talk about yourself in order to win a deal. Once you have done this, prepare another five-minute presentation about your company and its product or service, and again test it out.

In my opinion, marketing is one of the vital components of your business strategy. Never be embarrassed about the scope and scale of your marketing. Remember that in a new business, no one else is going to do it for you! This is also the case when you enter a partnership with colleagues.

Someone specifically has to own the marketing project and be enthusiastic to promote the ethos of the business. Never assume that someone else is dealing with marketing: get it agreed at the outset who is leading the role and get them (or you) to put together the marketing plan for the next three years. Create a specific 12-month plan as well. I suggest limiting the length of the second plan to 12 months at the outset because your marketing will need to be agile in its approach, taking advantage of opportunities as and when they arrive. For example, there could be a change in legislation or an upturn in a particular investment market.

What's the difference between *economies of scale* and *economies of scope*, and why is this important to your marketing strategy?

This was an important learning point for me, especially with regard to marketing. When applying *economies of scale* to marketing you are sending out a single message in bulk, such as a newsletter. This does work. Because of the volume being used, production of your marketing can be cheap and timely.

But what about taking the same message and rearranging it to re-use parts of your message elsewhere to amplify your message? This is an *economy of scope*. The same newsletter you wrote to take advantage of *economies of scale* may feature various newsworthy topics in your profession. You will have spent time checking these topics to ensure that they are relevant, compliant and above all, interesting.

Example of an economy of scope

- Create a 'blogspot' on your website and segment the topics from your existing newsletter. Then turn them into blogs on your website. You will know that Internet listing sites crave new content.

- Record a five-minute discussion about an interesting and topical subject with a colleague, friend or family member. Then podcast this on your website, or if you are more sophisticated, video it and 'vodcast' it. Watch your Internet rankings soar.

- Use social networking sites to discuss the same issue. However, make sure that it is both relevant and compliant for your regulatory authority, if you have one.

- Convert your newsletter into an article, and write to the press about the issues you are considering. Choose an issue that you are well qualified to talk about and are able to answer questions about.

By doing this, you have taken one newsletter and reinvented it in four other formats, giving the same informed message in very different distribution styles, increasing the potential for audience variation and penetration. With a little extra application, it is possible to diversify your message and distribute it into other areas, creating greater scope for your message to be heard by new prospects.

Once you are recognised as an *expert* in the topic selected, update your thoughts and understanding and repeat the process.

As an example, many television channels have used the same philosophy, broadcasting their standard channel, then a 'plus 1' model, as a new separate channel, just one hour forward. They then add a website distributing the same information. This creates three distribution models for the same message. It's both innovative and cost effective.

Marketing techniques have changed significantly in recent years and I have found that subtlety over 'in your face' promotion works best. Many financial service organisations (other than the banks) lack a shop window and many would not want one. Walk-in trade is not what we are about. Quality enquiries from good prospects are what you're looking for. When you have got your marketing right, these prospects will find you easily.

Create a target area, such as a town or village, district or county, based on your research into where you anticipate your clients will be. You might rely on your own local knowledge to do this, or use a postcode system. Then make sure that in this area your name is going to come up time and time again. Sponsor something — it could be a roundabout, a music recital, a Shakespeare play or you could even write a book — that will get you press coverage in your chosen location. Add to this your own personal networking and your effort is likely to be well received, over time. It also has the advantage of giving something back to the community that you serve.

Write to the media about what you are doing, again and again. Take the editor of the local newspaper or business magazine to lunch. Place an advert in your local 'rag' and ask for some editorial space in return. Get on to the radio to talk about the latest issue in your world. You are not *selling* anything, but you are showing knowledge and passion about your subject and that should be enough to get the enquiries rolling in.

The *timing* of your marketing is vital.

Referring back to your year's sales target, you have correctly divided your sales target up into months to ensure that you maximise peak performance. Your marketing campaign must coordinate with this sales strategy. If you were running a Christmas shop, you probably would not start your company's peak marketing campaign in July.

The same applies to financial services. You might build your campaign up to March/April/May and then regenerate it again to October/November. Don't waste effort and advertising costs in August and December, unless you are sponsoring something in the locality you are targeting to give back to their community.

Age ranges

You can also focus on age range and target your marketing accordingly.

We currently target the over 50s market. This is because we are focused on retirement planning and this is an obvious step. Our website, office and business need to reflect the age range we as a small organisation are trying to attract and retain: not too funky but still upbeat, professional and trustworthy.

However, if we were selling mortgages or life assurance, the natural client recruit for these products would be younger, perhaps 22-48, and the marketing style would have to value *their* ideals and needs.

Your proposition must recognise this and be reflected in the business or website names that you choose. 'Silver surfers' are usually just as dynamic as 22 year olds, but in a different way; you need to buy into the subtle differences of these dynamics to get your marketing message correct.

What is 'networking' about?

I am not sure I had heard the word *networking* about ten years ago. I had heard of *getting out there* and *chatting to people to get your name around*, but not networking. Networking is the least results-driven marketing I have ever come across. Some would argue that this is a weakness.

It must be said, however, that networking is very powerful when done well. Returning to the subject of your target market, there will be groups of likeminded people who meet informally at events to mingle and discuss their lives, their businesses and most importantly, their needs. Networking is about *getting involved* — and, to use the old adage, the more you put in, the more you get out.

Networking events are great for giving you practice at explaining succinctly what you do for a living. More importantly, they are an excellent way of finding out whom you can work with and what they can offer you. Concentrating on other people allows a subtle 'sell' of both yourself and your own offering.

As I've said before, *people* buy people and networking is a case in point. You will usually have less than five minutes to make an impact on someone. This is partly because you will want to move around the event to meet as many people as possible, and partly because your target will want to do the same. Never turn up to an event without a top pocket full of your own business cards, and never leave an event without a pocket full of everyone else's. You may want contact them afterwards.

Don't be embarrassed about moving around the venue and possibly cutting conversations short to change your prospect 'target'. You are there to meet and greet as many people as you can and this is an excellent and cheap way of getting your name around your chosen location. Remember that it will take time to filter your name out, and you will meet many interesting and varied folk in the process. You never know when a particular randomly met contact will come in handy.

Think about joining your local Chamber of Commerce, golf club or other local organisation, even your local political party. You never know where it will take you and whom you will meet. Some events will allow a speaker to spend 15 minutes extolling their virtues and their services. Make sure that you volunteer and that you get your slot.

Combine this networking process with your branding and other marketing initiatives and the overall proposition quickly starts to become compelling.

What's your brand?

To ensure success, you should have a distinctive logo or brand from the outset that people will remember. Even if they don't remember it, have your brand visible in sufficient volume around the selected area, so that they will be reminded.

Your brand should inspire confidence and trust, because people buy *brands*, just as they buy *you*.

Once you have your logo, don't change it for a while. It is my view that the buying public likes stability because, for some, it implies security — especially in the field of financial services. Branding is important; re-branding in the short term is not.

Assuming you have the choice of what to call your company, then include what you do in the name. For example, if you are a financial planner then call yourself a *financial planner*. Just using a name is unlikely to work at the outset because people will not know you from Adam.

Remember that it is possible to 'over-market' your product or service and this is to be avoided. Overdoing it erodes the hard earned rapport that you have built with the clients, prospects and introducers such as accountants, solicitors and actuaries. It is important to subtly keep the brand name in the forefront of the client's mind. You can do this with a quarterly newsletter or fund update and a Christmas card — but don't extend this to a bombardment of literature, emails and calls, even if the boss insists. And the boss in this case is Esther.

For marketing, you need energy and lots of it. It is an evolving process, not an advert. Marketing can be applied to anything; from you personally networking, to your company, to a procedure or promotion that you want to endorse. Marketing should be gentle, almost subliminal, and the constant application of your message over time will achieve a regular enquiry rate.

By placing an advert here, a blog there, a podcast over there, a newspaper article next week, a radio comment the week after, your message will gain traction. Then, duplicate the same material. Use the articles, blogs and record podcasts and post them on your website.

One marketing tactic is to have more than one website or offering, and compete against yourself with an alternative business offering under another product name. Rather than being ambiguous in your offering, this is designed to attract different sectors of the market that may have not used your services before, thus increasing your business's scope for opportunity and profit.

The adage that *if you are not sitting in front of a client they cannot buy from you* can be extended in this situation to the virtual world of the Internet. You might think that this is a contradiction and a mad suggestion — but detergent manufacturers have been doing this for years and it works.

In addition, it hauls you up the Internet rankings, which is also important.

You wouldn't leave your front door unlocked, so why leave your brand unprotected?

Once you create a strong brand you must protect it with a trademark. At some point it would be reasonable to want to sell your company and brand to extract the most value. Use a trademark agent to get your efforts tied down. It can prove an expensive protection but worth every penny.

Trademark agents are easy to find and I have added some details of a trade body in the Resources section.

Also, if you build a website brand, don't forget to protect this as well. If you operate your website as a *.co.uk*, buy the *.com* too. If you trade as a financial planner on a website called ***www.erniebloggs.co.uk***, then you should buy the *.com*, <u>and</u> also the 'financial planning' end, which would be ***www.erniebloggsfinancialplanning.co.uk*** and *.com*. As your brand grows in both distinction and status, it is vital to protect your investment.

Marketing mentors will bore you to tears about the importance of your website. They'll ask things like, 'Do you have one?' and 'What system does it run on?' In their defence, they have a serious point as the site should be considered as your shop window; without one, you look closed. It is your virtual brochure and should be as individual as you are.

Your website should state the obvious benefits of dealing with you and your company, along with your USP (unique selling point) to attract and promote enquiries. Keep the website updated, as an old website is nearly as bad as no website at all. An old and tired shop window will quickly put prospects and enquirers off approaching you; they will search for a more vibrant and up to date offering. You could be handing your competitors an advantage if they are more up to date than you on the Internet.

Make the *contact us* button or navigation bar as obvious and easy to access as possible because enquirer like to be directed to contact easily.

If you are building a web brand that could be serialised, then do this for yourself at the outset. The 'at the outset' bit is vital. What do I mean by this?

For example, if you run a financial advisers' office, you might have a unique and fun website, such as www. pensionsmadesimple.com (and the *co.uk* version of course). You realise that this may only attract pension enquiries and this would be a limiting factor, because pensions represent only a quarter of your total sales repertoire. What about investment sales? Start to build a brand range that you can expand into by buying www.investmentsmadesimple.com and, say, www.advicemadesimple.com. You now have a series of offerings that you can use either straight away or later, when you are ready to expand your overall brand before you sell your business — if you want to. Further details are available in the Resources section.

Assuming you use your website for marketing, remember to monitor who and what visitors are looking at. Try to use low cost web-based facilities to monitor your Internet business traffic, such as www.statcounter.com or Google AdWords Analytics — although others are available. Again, more details can be found in the Resources section.

Starting a business to exit it?

When you set up a business, your own company or practice, you usually put together a business plan and run with it. But think forward from this initial period. When are you going to *exit* the business?

I met a lady within our profession who wanted to understand how to move her career forward. We discussed offering her a job. I have a high regard for her (hence the job offer) but she sensibly started her own company. It was the right move for her *life junction*. She had good commercial experience, great rapport skills and industry qualifications. Why am I telling you this? Well, one of the very first questions that she asked me was, 'What's your exit strategy?' I was stumped.

'Well, I'm only forty, so I haven't given thought to an exit strategy!' I chirped. Bearing in mind that she was even younger than me, I could not see the validity of the question. However, she was way, way ahead of me. Don't forget the purpose of starting up a business is to provide income, lifestyle, stability and then, hopefully, an asset that can provide capital.

Answer the following question at regular intervals: *Is the company running you or are you running the company?* Be honest with yourself and adjust your actions accordingly.

What is your answer to the question *'When are you going to exit?'* Where will that be? How will you achieve your exit? And, most importantly, what will be the trigger for you to do it? If you are precious enough to believe you would never sell your baby, then get with it quickly. You are not a registered charity; that should be why you started your business in the first place. If you build a quality brand that has value, then you should capitalise on that value at the right time.

In my travels I have met a few main board PLC directors. I met a chairman who told me: 'Any shareholder who tells you they are not in it for a profit is a liar!' Strong words — but if you are the main shareholder in your business, then profit in the form of income or a capital sale should be a main objective.

This brings into focus the issue of building value into the fabric of your business to increase value, real or perceived, to create a greater capital value for its eventual sale. I believe that the quality of your outfit is key here, and that quality, the value you are going to sell, needs to be built into every element of your production and income.

Car makers have been doing this for years, creating niche quality brands that many people covet. You buy a car for a purpose, such as its speed or its load capacity, but the choice is a reflection of you, and this usually points to the values and qualities you hold as your own. That's the reason you pored over the company car list for so long.

The same is true of your business. When you put your company into the 'business sale showroom' and the prospective buyers come to 'kick your tyres' the decision process they use is likely to be similar. They will look for quality and want to know whether your business is a good fit.

Finally, don't sell when you are too old. Sell when you and the business are mature but still fresh, not when you and the business is in the last days of its best before date. Buyers will know what life stage you are at, and will pitch the offers they make accordingly. There is only so far you can develop a company before you are going to need external input from others to take your baby to the next level. Do you really want to have the same role in the same company all your life? You may be offered a consultancy to your old business. If you are good, the buyer will not want you competing with them in a couple of years' time by starting another new business.

All the effort you put in has been worthwhile, and your business is growing nicely. Will it stay that way?

Chapter 16 in a nutshell

Grow a strong, memorable and stable brand. People like brands they can recognise and trust. Branding is good, re-branding is not, unless the organisation is tired. Work your marketing constantly and with energy.

Having built your brand, protect it. Use a trademark agent. Protect your website brands by also securing the other variants, such as .co.uk and .com and .org.

Join your local Chamber of Commerce, golf club or other local organisation, even your local political party. Each organisation will take you to different opportunities each time.

17. You're now afloat
– but is your ship's rigging tight?

You started your business with a three year plan and, with many candles burnt at both ends, you are up and running and settling into your stride. As noted before, this confidence and sales success may come in the third year when you are starting to capitalise on the first two years of hard graft. This was the case for our company and it provoked the need for change.

Location, location, location . . . now, where have I heard that before?

With the original business plan written, we secured well-presented premises, which were also cheap for our start. The right premises are vital to any new business, as is a flexible property lease (because of some landlords). Remember, presentation is everything, from your polished shoes, to your clean office, to your letterhead. First impressions *do* count.

Business went well and we quickly began to outgrow our office. More clients means more files means more filing cabinets and, of course, less space. The magnolia walls and blue carpet floor of our highly functional but small office seemed to tighten. We had also taken on a part timer to help with administration as the duties of Esther and I became more involved. Comfortably squeezing in a third desk was going to be interesting and desk hopping is not my idea of fun. We looked around and after some time found perfect offices in the High Street. The new office felt good (the 'gut feel' I mentioned earlier) and we also knew that clients would feel good when signing up to our sales initiatives.

You remember how it goes: 'Sign here, here and here, please.'

But what's in a name and location? We had moved only 200 metres round the corner; surely it was not going to make that much difference because nothing else had changed, other than having 'High Street' in the address. No one could have ever convinced us how much difference a move like this would make.

We believed the new location we selected was almost perfect, and clearly we were right because greater levels of high calibre enquiries started coming in. The stature of the company has risen and with it productivity and the 'P' word, *profit!*

It pays not to be proud about location. I have a client who uses us purely because we are close to the good shops in the town and they can 'kill two birds with one brick.' And there was I, thinking he valued me for my industry qualifications and witty repartee!

Once you have got your new business running and are planning an expansion move, remember that a business address and its location can mean the difference between hard work and harder work. And when you do move, be sure to throw an opening launch party, inviting the press, your introducers, prospects and clients to the event, and get your picture splashed across as many publications as possible. It's a great marketing opportunity.

Add a notice to your website and your social networking sites to ensure the world knows what you and your company are up to — because good news, as well as bad, can travel fast. Vanity is good for publicity and good for profit. Note to self: enjoy the party!

Culling clients

You should be in business to make a profit. You want clients, not customers, and you want to focus on undertaking productive work, not wasting time.

In the process of running your company you will pick up some business that is a one-hit sales situation. The customer wants you to implement a change or buy a product for a specific purpose and that's it, nothing more. You are a conduit to an objective, rather than an adviser. This in itself is not a problem and don't be too proud to take the business if it is available.

However, take a step back from your sales work and remind yourself who is a client and who is a *customer*. You do not want to be spending valuable time and effort on marketing to someone who has gained all their value from you, and who has no intention of doing business with you again because they have already met all of their objectives.

An example might be a client who wants to implement a pension transfer for divorce purposes. They don't plan to get divorced regularly, they may not have wanted their pension split in the first place (preferring cash instead) and you are simply a person who can make the transaction for them with minimum fuss and effort.

I once had one of these cases where we won the business because we were close geographically to their solicitors, rather than because of our business offering. This was not an ideal situation; however, we secured the case and made a profit. But I don't lose sleep over the fact that they are never going to buy from us again.

It's nothing personal. If a customer is not going to buy again, then don't waste effort on him in the future. He won't mind. Once a one-off purchase is completed and settled, move these types of customer from 'active' clients to a 'dormant or inactive' category. Ensure that you keep the records, as required, and move on, focusing your attention on those that need your service regularly.

I referred to treating yourself and your business fairly in a previous chapter, and this is a simple way of keeping yourself focused on a quality sales process.

Let's switch the money off!

At this point, I feel like adding the old television warning of 'Don't try this at home, kids!', but you should. And when it comes to cash flow planning, it would also be nice to say, 'Here's one I made earlier,' but you can't.

Most companies need to diversify and adapt to survive and thrive. That might be because of variances in markets or trading conditions, or because of regulatory changes or requirements.

This is the same for any occupation and an example could be electricians. They now need a 'Part P Certificate' (introduced in 2005 for dwellings) to fit most things electrical in your house. An electrician might be brilliant and have years of experience but he cannot work legally without this certification. Many electricians have had to go back to college to pass this certification, to prove that their day-to-day work is correct and of a high standard. This may cause a short-term setback to their business but will be worthwhile in the long term.

Financial services advice is no different, with many companies moving from a commission model to a fee based model to become more transparent to both clients and regulators. This is also in order to meet proposed significant regulatory changes in future years. Personally, I believe this is a change for good, although I can vouch for the fact that the transition is hard work. Various industry 'experts' disagree with me on that point.

With the writing on the wall many quality financial advisers will have to make the switch to fee based work. But how?

Start by building some cash reserves in the business if you can, to cushion any short-termcash flow problems. And you *will* get a cash flow problem! This will usually manifest itself as a hole in the bank account. No one prepares you for this, so learn it here from me. In my first three months of starting a company, I met an accountant (who has subsequently become a client) who stated:

'I am not really interested in gross or net profit figures. I want to know the company cash flow position.

'A company is nothing without cash flow,' he confirmed. He was absolutely right.

To an extent, the economic recession is a cash flow problem, rather than a profit and loss position. A phrase in a song suggests of money that it makes the world go round and that the people who move this money are bankers; *your* bankers, to be precise.

When running a business, make sure you keep your bankers apprised of your cash flow position because they can help in both negative and positive cash flow positions. Your bankers like you, do not like surprises of any kind.

In the preparation time allowed to make a switch within any business, practise your new business approach. You may have always been comfortable with selling on a commission basis and you are now switching to fees. You have to become just as comfortable with selling fees because you are going to need to be confident in your presentation to clients and prospects.

When you go to a networking event, you will often be asked what profession you follow. You have thirty seconds to enlighten your enquirer about the benefits of your business and its charging structure, so be ready. Practise your new approach with your colleagues or family to make sure that your message is professional, clear and well practised.

Take your time to select your timing of any process switch in the business; assuming the timing of this change is within your control. In our case, I started late in the month of May. Why then? Because we had just completed our major sales months of the calendar year (as noted in the suggested sales target chart, although with different production figures!) and the sales pipeline was looking plump and healthy.

Check the quality of the sales in the pipeline at this time to ensure that the likely completions are realistic, without any potential for default. Having checked, we were satisfied that the quality of the pipeline business would tide us over the summer period. This time of year would probably be naturally quieter — although, as you know, past performance is not a guarantee of future performance! This would allow time for the implementation of the switch process to the new fee based model.

To start with, the cash flow gap lasted about three months starting in the August, three months after the process started in May. Be warned. It created a wave effect of cash in the modelling, with the benefit of actually creating a far stronger business model than the original commission based programme. We are now winning more clients and they enjoy the full transparency of the advice transaction.

It should also be noted that the completion time frame of the new business model extends out from the sales model. In providing financial advice, you might be creating a programme for a client over a 12 month period or longer. This may extend the time that the agreed remuneration is paid, because it is not reliant on a client commission sale.

Once you have made your change, then hold firm and stay with it. The pain will be worth it.

It's how much?

Is what you sell price sensitive? Or is it about people rather than price?

To some extent, the answer to the price part of the question has to be positive. Your offering has partly to be about cost — but possibly only to the limit of the parameters that *you* perceive. If you have confidence in the quality of your offering, and that the delivery of your message is not scripted to suit someone else's process, then you should be able to communicate the intrinsic value to the client of your offering and its benefits.

I know that the term 'benefit selling' is a piece of American jargon but its virtues are correct. As an example, a *feature* could be the tax efficient nature of a product providing greater final value. The *benefit* at retirement could be the ability to buy a bigger car or a better holiday when you get there. And if you can be comfortable, fluent and confident in your delivery, then the price issue reduces.

Consider experimenting with your pricing and ensure that the price parameters that you work within are profitable, even at their lowest level in the overall process. This will ensure that your charges experiment will only affect the level of profit that you achieve, rather than becoming an issue of whether your business survives or not.

This last statement makes the assumption that you know the level of income needed to achieve profitability. I assume here that you would have established this in the business plan that you achieved prior to starting off. If not, check this quickly.

Your charges and fees can be made in various formats. One easy way to demonstrate this division is to consider the initial sale fee and then the ongoing servicing fee that you may charge. Like the sale of a new boat or motorcycle, they have a 'sale price' and a different 'life cost' for the consumer, which takes into account the running of the vehicle. When dealers sell a vehicle at cost price, which they might do to maintain cash flow, then the dealer usually hopes to win the servicing business too, which will bring in more profit than the initial sale.

Most businesses can be coordinated like this, increasing or adjusting profit to achieve the deal in the shorter term but keeping the consumer buying in the longer term, creating an overall profit margin for the provider.

Establish where in the process you earn the income and subsequently profit, and adjust these parameters over time to see the effects on both profit and business volumes. This should allow you and your business to create an optimum model which works fairly for all parties involved.

In addition, look at payment methods and offer alternatives to the client to attract their business without, to any greater extent, affecting your cash flow. If it's a large case, you might offer to split the invoice over four quarters in a year, or into monthly payments, to make the 'price point' less onerous.

Try it; in many cases the results can be highly favourable and clinch the deal.

Buy into this change process personally, and get colleagues and supporters to agree to the change and promote their virtues — because, in this case, there are virtues. Talk to your business friends about the situation and their experiences because their input will be valuable. They may have encountered results that you have not envisaged, and may be able to guide you around any pitfalls to enhance your success.

Think about your business and accept the challenge of change when it appears over the horizon, because in this politically correct world that we live in, it surely will.

Chapter 17 in a nutshell

Don't forget that a good business address and its location can be the difference between hard work and harder work.

Cash flow is king in any business and as a business owner you must never take your eye off it! Check the bank account every day.

Know your profit margins on each sale you achieve, to allow you flexibility when it comes down to the negotiation, if required, of your fees. There is nothing worse than winning a case and then regretting the deal because it was not profitable.

18. From Spandau Ballet to Spandau Ballet

We have travelled through pension mis-selling, endowment scandals, the Personal Investment Authority (and its predecessors) and the 'big bang' in London, to increases in higher rate tax, the FSA and a significant recession — all in the course of one book.

The world does not stand still and I am sure more regulatory authority changes are afoot. I hope that my thoughts have helped you put in context some of the issues of the current economic situation, provided guidance on moving your career forward and assisted you in understanding that we have been here before — although the situation has varied and the opportunities are different.

You have read my personal journey of learning, noting successes and, to coin a phrase, 'areas for development' as well as what you might need to consider in your own journey of discovery.

We have gone full circle, encompassing the years 1985 to date. We have gone from the vital Geneva summit of Presidents Gorbachev and Reagan in 1985 to the modern reality of the credit crunch, MPs' expenses, and the development of the virtues and business possibilities of the Internet.

The possibilities for you, your business and your prospects are limited only by the limits of your own aspirations. I hope that, this work has provided you with the inspiration to strive further in your career. Push the possibilities of your remit and think outside the box in ways that will expand your horizons.

In music, we have travelled through pop and the new romantic era with Kajagoogoo, Rick Astley, the Human League and Spandau Ballet to . . .well, much the same music in fact. There is something strange, yet rather enjoyable, about all these band comebacks. Or is it just me? At least the quality of the sound is better on my MP3 player than the cassette in my 1980s 'Walkie' stereo that would eat my newest album and unravel itself at every opportunity. I wonder if the oversized frilly white shirts, heavy makeup and moody street scenes will make it onto our screens again?

From an economic perspective, some people argue that the recession was caused by the UK's switch into financial services and other service based industries to fuel the economy, at the beginning of the 1980s, at the expense of manufacturing industries. Could the reality of this situation possibly be that this move *deferred* a recession for a lot longer and deeper than would have otherwise been the case for the UK?

This leads on to the Government's programme of *quantitative easing*. Some cynical souls say that this is simply adding a few noughts to the Government's bank balance so that they can go and buy financial assets, creating income into the system. Some refer to it as 'printing money'. I would provide you with a full explanation of how quantitative easing works, if indeed it does work at all, but you'd lose the will to live long before I finished it!

This raises the question: where next for the UK economy and its workforce?

It is now being mooted that the UK government hopes we will become a base for expertise in green technologies, supporting the world in its thrust to slow global warming. I hope the reality of this is the case — but I also hope that any growth in this industry is sustainable and not just another government initiative to keep the economy afloat.

What have we learned?

UK financial services and its advice process offer great opportunities both to individuals and to corporations. It is also an inspiring, innovative and invigorating profession as long as you control it, rather than your role controlling you.

There is nothing more invigorating than being locked in negotiation with a client about their innermost feelings, desires, financial aspirations and needs — and providing robust solutions to these. Where else can you achieve this? I don't know of any other profession where you can do this day in and day out, five days a week, 48 weeks a year (allowing for holidays).

Was my journey worth the effort? Good question. The clients continue to be tremendous and I would like to thank them again as they are the lifeblood of the profession. We know so much about many of them, and they know much less about us! This is a huge responsibility and one to be respected and cherished.

I know I do.

Change is coming

I believe that being commission driven does not do the reputation of the financial services advice industry any favours.

The many true professionals among us are undertaking sterling work to correct the industry's somewhat tarnished reputation, to innovate and inspire. Long may their work continue and I salute them for their tireless endeavours. It will be interesting to see whether the blueprint changes prepared by the FSA to the UK financial services distribution models in the next decade will actually succeed in improving the public's understanding of financial advice.

And what of the future for you and me and financial advice in the High Street?

First of all, will there be a future for your average financial adviser? Probably not. Or, as an alternative, they will be working within a non-independent sales environment offering lower risk products for a large High Street outlet. There is nothing wrong with this.

I also believe that well qualified and experienced financial planners will reap many rewards — but that this service will only attract high value clients who can afford the luxury of true financial planning.

We may end up with a three-tiered service offering in the UK:

- The *have nots*, who were never going to be affluent, buying products rather than advice

- The *haves*, who are rather modest in asset size and income

- The *large haves*, well advised and with the majority of the wealth

The 80:20 sales rule may apply, with 20 per cent of clients providing 80 per cent of the income because they hold 80 per cent of the wealth.

The Internet will also have a growing role in the provision of financial advice in the UK and Europe, mainly focusing on the prospects of the middle wealth band. This may contract the market for the banks at one end of the marketing spectrum, and for those that profess only to operate at the top end of the market.

A different world — not better or worse, just different

The recession that we have endured will linger and then go, as recessions have done in decades gone by.

Comparisons have been made between recent recessions and the Great Recession of the late 1920s and 1930s.

Our current situation may take longer to improve. In my opinion, the UK economy was overdue a recession. It comes as no surprise that this economic crisis is a rather angry beast, different from that of the early 1980s and 1990s.

Many people are convinced that this recession is led by the banks and this statement has some traction. However, the reality is that the recovery when it comes will *also* be led by the banks, by them injecting both capital and profits back into the system to put us on track for recovery.

Bankers are often characterised as greed-driven individuals. This is not the case and never has been. They are clever people doing difficult work for the benefit of their organisations, and they undertake this work with rigour — despite their bad press.

The levels of government borrowing and nationalisation across the globe are far higher than were ever anticipated, and will mean that the burden of debt for many economies will linger for decades to come. Sadly, the UK has been highlighted as one of these economies.

I have met many clients who are concerned, not for themselves, not even to a reduced extent for their children, but for their grandchildren's fiscal future. Their underlying fear is that future generations will not be able to enjoy what they themselves have taken for granted — such as employment, a home, pension and good health care.

The problem that this recession is now revealing is that

all this may be the case, not because it's a recession, but because of the resulting debt burden being used to correct the recession which will slowly recovery.

I believe that the world will be a different place when this economic crisis is over. Not better or worse, just *different*.

Do not misunderstand me: some individuals and organisations will still make obscene profits in the future, and large yachts will still bob around in the harbours and playgrounds of the CEOs and celebrities.

It will be at the margins that we will see the true difference, for what some have referred to as the *mass affluent*. The comfort of the Final Salary pension scheme, enjoyed by the baby boomers, will disappear.

Evidence of this is already available. Taxation, either direct or indirect, will rise to service the government debt that has been accumulated to pull us out of recession. This extra burden may well fall on our children and grandchildren. I believe that the US politician, John McCain, referred to this as 'generational theft', and his apt comment seems prophetic. The banks and lending institutions will be very much more cautious in their lending policies in the future, meaning fewer loans and mortgages being granted to the more affluent applicants.

But this raises the question of whether the economy we experienced before was realistic or an accident waiting to happen (and which has now happened). One possible consequence of this recession is that future generations will stay at home longer, renewing the potential for extended families, rather than the nuclear families that we have seen over the last 30-40 years.

The baby boomers retiring now could see their children becoming *Baby Gloomers* in the future, supporting children at home into their twenties, thirties and even forties — at the same time as supporting older generations. I am describing a financial sandwich, with the present fortysomethings as the filling. It does not sound very appetising.

I am reminded by others that this was the same case 50-60 years ago in a world recovering from war.

When this recession started, I mused with a young staff member about the bad old days when the oil crisis came to a head in 1973. I told her about the three-day working week, although, bearing in mind I was only six at the time, all I could remember was walking home from school with my brothers in the dark streets because power cuts were the norm, varying in lengths.

The power cuts were required frequently during the week, but the one we all remembered was the loss of power between six o'clock and nine o'clock sharp on a Sunday evening. My mother would make sure that her boys were washed, fed and all other ablutions finished, and that we were gathered in a safe place, which usually meant an early bedtime, in time for the power to go off.

I always feel I sound like the Monty Python sketch when commenting on that oil crisis, saying: 'And you tell the kids of today and they don't believe you' — but that situation was only 35 years ago. My young colleague thought I was spinning a yarn until she Googled it. She was horrified. It is an excellent reminder of how the world has changed, and that the nature of change will continue to evolve in ways we would never imagine.

Great opportunity

Change creates opportunity in whatever walk of life you come from or work in, so don't resist it, and be an early adopter of your opportunities. People who recognise change and work with it will shine, and this becomes self-perpetuating in generating prosperity.

What opportunities will there be for those planning to join the financial advice profession?

I think that their prospects are good if they see it as a *profession*, rather than a job. High levels of professional qualifications will become the norm, rather than an unnecessary evil, and the sooner these studies are undertaken the better. Also, I recommend that you embrace the compliance and regulatory regimes that surround us, because they will not go away. They are there for your protection as well as for the clients' benefit, so learn and understand them well, and they will give you a smoother ride — both now and in the longer run.

The informed requirements from clients, to have more access and control in the allocation of their funds via the Internet, will increase. This is a natural progression towards a more American-style system, where many people have full access to their own investments and watch them closely.

With financial education improving for the public, with some money planning being taught in the state education system, we will move more into an advisory role, rather than concentrating on product sales, as clients execute their own deals and purchases directly with providers or online with our guidance.

When computers first became prevalent in the early 1980s, and Lord (Alan) Sugar was selling us processors by the lorry load, I am sure not even he guessed that by 2010 we would be strapped to computers wherever we go. We are never out of touch, with WiFi in nearly every street — and this coverage will only improve with the 4G telecommunications network just around the corner.

I love going on holiday and lazing on a beach. Sadly, so does my computer Netbook, with emails and mobile phone linked to my office, clients and the financial services world as a whole. My beach lounger by the pool looks like the Jodrell Bank communications station by the time I have laid out my towel. I have learned from my previous technology errors, although I seem not to be alone; many others, mainly men, are also tapping out their emails and text messages.

What else we can achieve online? How long will it be before you can get full financial advice online without the need for a meeting? This is something that financial advisers will have to consider, and adapt to quickly, to maintain market share and profitability.

And what of your motivations, your satisfiers and dis-satisfiers? If nothing else, this book will at least confirm that you are not alone, that others have shared the joys, experiences and frustrations that most of us have. From here on, it will all be down to the way that you deal with these issues, putting them into perspective and using your learning, to take advantage and to achieve success.

I'm sure you can bring to mind the one thing that your most memorable manager, director or colleague used to do, that you would love to have changed in your employment past. Cherish that memory, that burning issue, that was so wrong. And as you run around plying your trade, make sure that you learn from that wrong point and put it right. There is nothing worse than learning something bad . . . and then repeating it in your new role! Do something different, something innovative, refreshing, even uplifting; you should know how to do it now.

I believe that the financial services industry — and the advisory market in particular — is full of innovation with energetic, positive and capable people who will be able to step up to the mark and enhance this rapidly changing and dynamic environment. Whatever you do or try, enjoy it!

My objective with this book was to share some of my experiences and demonstrate the good, the bad, the ugly and the amusing, to impress upon you, the reader, that success is there for the taking. All you have to do is focus your energy intelligently. It is not an easy road and there are no quick fixes available.

The challenge to you is to take the journey, *your* journey, to the next level. I hope you will be one of these leaders, our leaders, in the twenty-first century.

After all of these thoughts, experiences and incidents, I return to the question I first posed myself at the beginning of this chapter: 'Was the journey worth it?'

Yes, you bet it was!

Chapter 18 in a nutshell

Your own evolution will never stop but your attitude to these life changes will. Learn to use your experiences to your advantage.

Prepare for a different economic and financial world. Learning something bad or how not to do something is not a problem as long as you don't go and replicate it elsewhere.

I return to the question, Was the journey worth it? Yes, you bet it was! Seize every opportunity and wring the juice out of it. It is yours for the taking.

Resources

References:

Frederick Irving Herzberg (1923–2000) 1968 publication *One More Time, How Do You Motivate Employees?* (Harvard Business Review Classics)ISBN-10: 1422125998

Abraham Maslowin his 1943 paper *A Theory of Human Motivation. AH Maslow* (1943) Originally Published in *Psychological Review*, 50, 370-396.

Napier University, Edinburgh, Financial Services BA (Hons) Degree /
www.napier.ac.uk

Learning and Industry

- *The Financial Services Authority (FSA)*

The Financial Services Authority (FSA) is an independent non-governmental body, given statutory powers by the Financial Services and Markets Act 2000.

Website: www.fsa.gov.uk

- *The Chartered Insurance Institute:*

Dedicated to promoting higher standards of competence and integrity through the provision of relevant qualifications for employees at all levels and across all sectors.

Website: www.cii.co.uk

- *Standards International:*

A leading certification body accredited to certify BS ISO 22222:2005 – the quality standard for providing personal finance services.

Website: www.standardsinternational.co.uk

- *The Institute of Financial Planning:*

The UK professional body of those committed to the development of the multi-discipline profession of Financial Planning.

Website: www.financialplanning.org.uk

- *The Personal Finance Society (The PFS):*

Membership of the PFS gives you access to everything you need to plan and develop your career in financial services.

Website: www.thepfs.org

- *The ifs School of Finance*

The *ifs School of Finance* provides education to financial services professionals.

The *ifs School of Finance* is a registered charity incorporated by Royal Charter

Website: www.ifslearning.ac.uk

- *Napier University, Edinburgh*

Edinburgh Napier is one of the top ten universities in the UK for graduate employability.

Website: www.napier.ac.uk

Commerce

- *The British Chamber of Commerce:*

The ultimate business network.

Website: www.britishchambers.org.uk

- *Statcounter*

A free yet reliable invisible web tracker, highly configurable hit counter and real-time detailed web stats.

Website: www.statcounter.com

- *Google AdWords Analytics*

You can display your ads on Google and our advertising network to increase Internet traffic.

Website: www.google.co.uk/AdWords

- *The Institute of Trade Mark Attorneys*

The UK professional body dedicated to the protection of trademarks.

Website: www.itma.org.uk

Charity

- *The Association for Spina Bifida and Hydrocephalus*

ASBAH is the leading UK registered charity (Registered Charity No: 249338) providing information and advice about spina bifida and hydrocephalus. A donation from the sale of each book will be given to our chosen charity, the Association for Spina Bifida and Hydrocephalus.

Website: www.asbah.org

Churchouse

- *More about Keith Churchouse and his companies at:*

www.churchouse.com or www.planmypension.co.uk

About the Author

Having been in the financial services industry for a quarter of a century and qualified to a high level within UK retail financial services, Keith set up Churchouse Financial Planning Limited with Esther Dadswell in 2004. A Chartered Financial Planning Company in Guildford, Surrey  the company offers independent bespoke advice to clients and enquirers. This ranges from pensions and retirement planning, including tax planning, through to investments, wealth management, business and health and life insurance protection planning. Keith also completed a BA (Hons) degree in Financial Services in 2007 with Napier University and became a Fellow of the Personal Finance Society in December 2007. In 2008, using Standards International, he was the 4th person in the UK to achieve ISO 22222 Certified Financial Planner status, the British Standard for Personal Financial Planners.

Pensions in divorce is an additional specialism. Having been divorced himself, Keith is a Resolution accredited Financial Neutral.

Keith has demonstrated that he is keen on innovation in the UK retail financial services industry, and as a result he has created two new websites in addition to his main business, Churchouse Financial Planning. Now you don't need to visit a financial adviser to receive a full financial report as this can be done online.

These services are:

www.advicemadesimple.com and www.planmypension.co.uk

Churchouse Financial Planning Limited has been Highly Commended at the Gold Standards Awards in both 2007 & 2008.

He has made regular and significant press comment in the local and national press and has frequently been interviewed on the radio over the last five years.

He has an active social media presence and can be found on Linkedin.com and Twitter as onlinefinancial. In addition, Keith tries to have a life outside work, and very much enjoys writing books, art, keeping fit by cycling and exercise and scuba diving.

He practises what he says and Churchouse is a Registered Trademark of Churchouse Financial Planning Limited.

Finally, Keith is proud to be the current President of the Guildford Committee (2009/2010) of the Surrey Chambers of Commerce, an active and highly successful business network in Surrey.

Bulk Order Form

Sign Here, Here and Here!...

If you would like to place a bulk order (minimum 10 books) for this book then this can be achieved with a direct discount of 25% per book (plus postage and packaging).

Item	Each	Quantity	Amount
Sign Here, Here and Here!...	£7.49		
Postage (per 10 books)			**£15.00***
	Total	£	

Please make cheque and payments payable to:
Churchouse Consultants LLP

Your details:

Name :	
Address :	
Postcode :	
Contact Number/Email :	

Post your order to:
Hadleigh House, 232 High Street, Guildford, Surrey, GU1 3JF

Our contact details for further information:

Tel: ***01483 578800***   Fax: 01483 578864
Email: ***info@churchouse.com***

www.signherehereandhere.co.uk

Sign here, here and here
Hadleigh House,
232 High Street,
Guildford,
Surrey,
GU1 3JF